C000070479

Exploring
the Palace of
the Peacock

30150 020939838

Joyce Sparer Adler

Exploring the Palace of the Peacock

Essays on Wilson Harris

Joyce Sparer Adler

Edited by Irving Adler

Foreword by Janet Jagan

EDINBURGH UNIVERSITY LIBRARY

UNIVERSITY OF THE WEST INDIES PRESS
Jamaica • Barbados • Trinidad & Tobago

University of the West Indies Press
1A Aqueduct Flats   Mona
Kingston 7   Jamaica

© 2003 by The University of the West Indies Press
All rights reserved. Published 2003

07 06 05 04 03   5 4 3 2 1

CATALOGUING IN PUBLICATION DATA

Adler, Joyce Sparer
Exploring the palace of the peacock: essays on Wilson Harris /
Joyce Sparer Adler; edited by Irving Adler; foreword by Janet Jagan.
p. cm.
Includes bibliographical references.

ISBN: 976-640-140-3

1. Harris, Wilson – Criticism and interpretation. 2. Harris,
Wilson. The Palace of the peacock. I. Adler, Irving.

PR9320.9.H3 P334 2003   813.2

Cover illustration: Isaiah James Boodhoo, Foliage (1988).
Collection of the University of the West Indies.

Book and cover design by Robert Harris.
Set in Adobe Garamond 11/15 x 27

Printed in Canada.

Contents

Foreword

Janet Jagan

I was most happy to receive a request from Irving Adler to write a few words for the book he is publishing of Joyce Sparer Adler's essays on Wilson Harris.

I have known both Joyce Sparer and Wilson Harris; my acquaintance with Mr Harris goes back more than fifty years. It was during the exhilarating period of the 1940s and early 1950s when my late husband, Cheddi Jagan, and I and others were gathering forces and ideas and building ideals to begin the long struggle for independence of the then British Guiana.

At our home in Laluni Street, Georgetown, a few years after Cheddi's return from dental studies in the United States and my arrival after our marriage in 1943, we met many young Guyanese and used to have frequent talks, exchanges of views and books, all leading to revolutionary thoughts and preparations for action.

Wilson Harris, the surveyor and poet, and Martin Carter, another budding poet, came over in the evenings to Laluni Street and read their poems to us. These were heady days full of activity, passion and resolve. (Martin Carter later became Guyana's national poet.)

Wilson invited me to join his surveying team in the interior, which I accepted. It was then that I understood that the beauty, mystery and profound quiet of the interior greatly influenced what was to be his life as a writer. It was already creating the poet in him, which would later lead to his creative powers as a novelist.

Joyce Sparer came to Guyana at another important and most difficult period in the struggles of the People's Progressive Party led by Cheddi Jagan for independence and the betterment of its people. The 1960s were haz-ardous times. The Central Intelligence Agency was interfering in the inter-nal affairs of British Guiana and participating in a dangerous campaign to destabilize the elected government of Premier Cheddi Jagan.

Dr Jagan, in his vision of a free Guyana, sought to establish a university. With few resources and a hostile opposition, re-enforced by the Central Intelligence Agency, he went ahead and started the university at Queen's College, the premier high school, using the building after hours. Joyce Sparer was one of the courageous, self-sacrificing persons who joined the faculty of the newly inaugurated University of Guyana. She stayed in Guyana for five years, teaching at the university and living through the very difficult times, never losing her cool or her deep interest in the country, which finally achieved independence in 1966. It was during this time that she became interested in the works of Wilson Harris who had gone to live in England, where he still resides.

Wilson Harris has to his name a number of books which have been rec-ognized for their depth and penetration to the core of the meaning of his homeland. That Joyce Sparer reviewed and closely examined his works is a credit to her discernment, as Wilson Harris has never been a popular writer, too intellectual, much too deep, too profound for his novels to be bestsellers.

Joyce Sparer made a positive contribution to Guyana, first in helping to establish the University of Guyana, then as a teacher and later in recogniz-ing the worth of one of Guyana's leading writers.

Wilson Harris

An Autobiographical Essay

I live now in Essex with my wife Margaret. It is some thirty-odd years since I emigrated from Guyana, South America, to the United Kingdom. I was thirty-eight when I left British Guiana (as Guyana was then called) in 1959. An English friend tells me that the marvellous glow one sees sometimes – particularly at the end of the day – across the rolling Essex countryside is known as the East Anglian light. He claims that this radiance is due to a pattern of rainfall that is adequate but not excessive in this corner of England and also to the open vistas and skyscape that run from the sea miles away on the distant East Anglian coast of Norfolk.

All this is of great interest to me for landscape/skyscape/riverscape/ seascape (and their intermingled bearing on each other which transcends immediate locality) have been a living text – if I may so put it – in the way I read and reread the elements (as if the elements were a book) when I lived in South America and travelled from the Atlantic coastlands into the heartland of the Guyanas.

Now I sometimes find that the rolling Essex countryside reminds me of an aspect of the savannahs of the Guyanas. I dream of the survey expeditions I led there and into the rainforests as a young man for fifteen years or so.

Peculiar as it may seem, those expeditions through the coastlands into the rainforests have enriched my appreciation of the northern world. Likewise my experience of East Anglian light gives to memory's return to the Guyanas a rhythm and counterpoint, a spatiality, that affects, for instance, the narrative shape and imageries in the passage below that comes from my latest published novel *The Four Banks of the River of Space,* which appeared in 1990.

> Our guide was signalling to us. The mouth of the trail had been cleared and we climbed and entered the Bush. The fantastic, planetary greenheart trees rose into marvellous silvery columns on every hand. Clothed in water-music. The trail was narrow. We walked in single file. The cracked silvery veil of greenheart possessed the texture of slow-motion rain falling within the huge Bell of a still Waterfall in which whispering leaves of fluid sound ran up into veil within veil of Shadow-organ gloom towards the highest reaches of the Forest and the slit of the Sky far above. Subtle fire-music.
>
> I had never before seen the shining bark of greenheart columns in this slow-motion raining light (nor the Sky clothed in frail ribbons of fire-music within the lofty gloom of a Bell) in all my remembered Dream of Forests I had travelled in my youth. How young was I, how old was I? We had entered it seemed – the Macusi guide first, Penelope second, Ross third, I last – an innermost chamber of the magical Waterfall beneath god-rock. It encompassed the globe, the ancient world, the modern world. As if the Waterfall had been uplifted from the river and transferred within us in the music of space, around us in Shadow-organ imperceptible (not wholly imperceptible for we were aware of it) dance of genesis. (From *The Four Banks of the River of Space*, pp. 132–33)

There was a large black trunk in my mother's bedroom which she opened for the first time in my presence on the day the news came that my stepfather had disappeared (presumed drowned) in the rivers and rainforests of Guyana. The year was 1929. I was eight years old.

My stepfather's death or disappearance was the second crucial bereavement my mother suffered in six years. My father had died suddenly in 1923, and my memories of him were therefore quite naturally void or hollow, though on seeing the contents of the large open trunk he seemed strangely alive in my aroused imagination because of books of his my mother held up, a photograph to which she pointed in which he stood between two companions, and a horse carven from a greenheart tree.

A subconscious thread or connection was woven then with the South American heartland of the Guyanas into which I was to lead many survey expeditions as a young man. The impact of the forests and savannahs on those expeditions was to become of profound value in the language of the fictions I later wrote. My stepfather's disappearance in that immense interior when I was a child was the beginning of an involvement with the enigma of quests and journeys through visible into invisible worlds that become themselves slowly visible to require further penetration into other invisible worlds without end or finality. All this was to loom in the drafts and revisionary scope of poems and novels I embarked upon in the 1950s. The heartland of South America was as remote in the early and mid-twentieth century to my relatives and friends as if it existed on Mars.

In 1929 – the year of the opening of the trunk – we were living in Georgetown (the capital of British Guiana). We had moved there from New Amsterdam (the other township on the coastlands some sixty miles away) in 1923. My father's estate had yielded enough for us to buy some property. But economy and prudence were needed, indeed essential. My father had been a successful businessman – particularly in the insurance field – but had entertained lavishly and run a chauffeur-driven car.

The shocking news of my stepfather imbued my mother – I was to learn later – with a conviction of bondage to fate. She felt herself fated to bereavement. Yet she retained in some degree a rebellious mind. She longed to travel, to go abroad, to leave the country, but circumstances made this impossible. When I emigrated to the United Kingdom in 1959 – eight years after her death – I felt the shadow of her approval. I was doing in a sense what she had desired in the late 1920s after losing two husbands.

I had just come in from cycling, lifted the bike up the stairs into the gallery of the house, when I heard what had happened. Even now after all these years I remember someone passing on the road singing "Gal me lover letter loss". It was an old river song. And I thought he dived into the river to find it and would never come back! The bike was a gift from him I had received on Christmas Day, 1926. The wonder of glittering wheels, the shining machine, have never entirely left me. Memory is enriched by shadows of ecstasy, Christmas ecstasy. He had wheeled me around the drawing room and into the bedroom where my mother now stood three years later beside the open trunk. Those three years from 1926 (the shadow of the bike) to 1929 (the year of the drowned man in the river) are an eternity.

As such it makes vivid the day of all days my mother opened the trunk and revealed to me its contents. She was weeping to break her heart. "They belong to *your* father," she cried, "the books, the horse." I felt grief and limbo yet light as a feather as if I were still being wheeled around the room on Christmas Day.

"They belong to your father," she repeated. A peculiar and a positive statement! Peculiar rebellion against fate? She was confused, distraught. My father was no longer here to own anything. And yet he was closer than he had ever been as I touched the books and the horse. There was reproach in my mother's voice directed at my vanished stepfather. She was reproaching him for abandoning her. *My* father would never have left her had he lived. She was confused. I was confused by a tide of emotion within her. Confused by memory's trunk, memory's open grave it seemed. She turned and left the room abruptly.

So little one knows about oneself. So much one is afraid to acknowledge. The moment of birth, of issuing from a woman's body, lies in a void. The birth of the imagination may terrify but it lies in some degree within a theatre of recollection. A realm enriched by uncertainties. Uncertainty, yet one touches the threads of the gestation of idea and vision by which unconscious memory erupts into the subconscious and conscious body and mind. In my latest published novel, the character Anselm retraces his steps to arrive at a capacity for revisionary judgements of the nature of reality within and without himself. He is told by Canaima, his guide, that such revisions make him "a medium of the dance" of time. Make him also the "carnival heir of the dance". Anselm is astonished. He had never seen himself in the light of a carnival heir and he records in his book of dreams that the shock of such disclosure leads him to contemplate alternative or parallel existences in himself. How strange is one to oneself? How many quantum strangers does one bear in oneself?

My first acquaintance with Homer's *Iliad* and *Odyssey* arose from the books in my father's trunk. Ulysses returned to his home, to his wife, to his son, disguised as a beggar, after twenty long years, ten on the plains of Troy culminating in the belly of the great wooden horse (the womb or foetal masquerade it provided the Greeks to outwit the Trojans), ten in foreign lands and upon the ocean wave. As I look back across the seas of time into the harbour of my childhood, it is not easy to disentangle the impact the Ulyssean beggar made on me, when I read the *Odyssey* with my mother's help, from an encounter I had with a Georgetown beggar a block or so away from our home. I came upon the Georgetown beggar the very year my stepfather disappeared. We lived in a good and quiet neighbourhood, and it was unusual to come upon beggars so close to home.

He was leaning against a red-flame flowering tree that grew on a parapet against a canal. Dusty. Ill-kempt. But his face and eyes upset me most of all. They looked so porous yet masklike. When I got home I could not eat. I saw those extraordinary, unsettling features on my plate on the dining table. Nausea, hollowness, engulfed me. I lost all appetite. Hollowness. But a sensation of being sculpted arose in that hollowness, shaped within, born to imagine, to visualize, strangers at the gate of the self.

Across half-a-century and more a shadowy surfeit, sickness, emptiness returns to instil traces of my encounter with the beggar. The fabric of his face upon a floating tide of sorrow is stitched into Homer's beggar within a tapestry of gestating vision . . . .

This is December 1991 as I write this essay. I look back into the body of a century and am aware of the difficulty of pinning down the origins of imaginary identity one shares with others, those one meets on the street who are real yet unreal, others who are equally problematic but real even though they come from an ancient world and from the dusty covers of a book; from the shelf of a library or from a grave, from one's father's trunk, from a river or an ocean.

The age of five is a shadow in the past but inexpressibly real. The age I floated upon the saddle of a bike and the ground seemed to tilt. The age in which I was initiated into the terrors of school. The age in which I was part of a shadowy congregation witnessing Latin theatre, the Stations of the Cross, the Pietà.

It happened this way. Next to the school was a Catholic cathedral established by the Portuguese in British Guiana in the 1920s. They were an influential minority at the time in the heterogeneous population of the Guyanas. The school and church were in Main Street. My mother had misgivings for – unlike my stepfather – she was not a Catholic. She was Congregationalist. My stepfather, who was of mixed Portuguese descent, was a strong Catholic. He chose the school. I felt frozen, unable to move, as I stood in a stream of indifferent bodies and faces pouring into classrooms, but was helped by my stepfather's niece, a tall, thin, gentle girl, who introduced me to the head-mistress. It was the Easter term in 1926 when I joined the school. And on Good Friday we were led by the headmistress into the cathedral. I watched the stations of the cross and felt the wooden Christ come alive when he was taken down into the arms of his mother. It was not wood I saw but the life of sculpture metamorphosed into a mystery of flesh-and-blood.

I am not myself a Catholic. The dogmas of the church, its rituals, its infal-libility, are coercive and unhelpful to me. But its music and the descent of the imagination into the life of sculpture were poignantly active that Good Friday afternoon in the reality of living objects and in the beauty of the sacred. Something in me that was half-frozen, half-fluid child, foetal spirit, susceptible to metamorphosis, responded to the spaces of a carnival theatre, carnival wood, carnival masks, the birth of associations imaginary and real. A few years later – after my stepfather's disappearance – I began to read the *Odyssey* with my mother's help. We read it together. I read of the Trojan horse. But it revolved in my mind and took on quite different proportions. For I saw it in the light of my own father's horse carven from a tree in the Guyana rainforests. I was in it, secreted within it, a splinter of "mother-horse, father-horse", a splinter in an inimitable cathedral of reality that threatens to enclose, to dominate, but also brings a taste of a dialogue with truth beyond coercion, a dialogue with the living arts of freedom one pays dear to exercise, so dear it is as if blood oozes from an axed tree, the radiance of the sun from the soil of memory.

> The Portuguese were renowned for the Carnival theatre they staged at Easter. The Good Friday Christ was nailed into, then taken from, the cross. The painted blood on his hands and feet, and in his side, seemed astonishingly real. I was struck, how-ever, less by the painted blood than by the gloom and shadow, the radiance and daz-zle, of glass windows arching up to the roof of the world. I was in the mutuality of

the divine, I was in mother-horse, I was in father-glass, father-horse, mother-glass, I ascended, descended, into a mysterious constellation of evolutionary spaces. (From *Carnival,* p. 122)

That passage appears in the novel *Carnival* and it invokes the seed of *Latin* theatre in which I was immersed at the age of five some sixty years earlier in the colony of *British* Guiana; a seed that caught the light of the descent of the imagination into objects that seemed to me then (and now) mysteriously potent and alive. One may not remember the hour of one's birth but the livingness of glass and wood and sacred space is a surrogate dimension of emergence from a womb of flesh-and-blood into the body of the mind. That surrogate body with its spatial antennae reaches into unconscious memory of light and darkness in the hour one was born, subconscious intimacy with the density and fragility of things one touches as if they grow out of one's fingertips.

Perhaps it is now clear that this autobiographical essay is, at one level, a retracing of my steps backwards into the past with the help of linkages in the fictions I have written. At another level it is a quest for "father-glass, mother-glass" in which particles of memory accumulate again into reflections of the mind's grasp of a procession of objects and masks that are native to the birth of vision and inimitably alive.

I stressed "*Latin* theatre on a Good Friday in *British* Guiana" a moment ago in order to illumine the diverse and paradoxical roots of my colonial heritage. I myself am not of Portuguese descent as my stepfather was. But there was an object-kinship between us. The wheeled machine he gave me was touched by the riddling light of Christmas ecstasy even as the painted Christ in the cathedral was born of Good Friday theatre. All these extremities of marvel and touch, the trade of things truly given, truly accepted, become the realization of a thread that runs through his blood and mine. Kinship is the realization of the object-miracle of life that has its roots in old and new worlds encapsulated in a box, or a book, or a cross, or a pattern of technology that illumines a shared passion rather than ideological greed. The object-miracle is alive also within diverse step or dance. The 1920s and 1930s were decades when masked dancers of African descent danced through the city on tall stilted amazing limbs. Special holidays were set aside for such dances.

They too were family – they subsisted upon a thread of metamorphosed object-kinship in that their flesh-and-blood was living sculpture in the dance. They were daubed sometimes with Hindu motifs – perhaps dancers of Indian descent were amongst them – as if to announce a shared dynasty of festival with Lord Shiva of Asian/Indian epic.

I knew that my father who had died when I was two was of mixed blood but I lost touch with his relatives, so that my family tree on his side remains obscure. The carven horse in his grave (so it seemed) of a trunk that my mother opened was threaded into Homer's giant horse when I read the *Odyssey* as a child, but it was also to be resurrected many years later and to be ridden by the character Donne in my first published novel, *Palace of the Peacock*.

> A horseman appeared on the road coming at a breakneck stride. A shot rang out suddenly, near and yet far as if the wind had been stretched and torn and had started coiling and running in an instant. The horseman stiffened with a devil's smile, and the horse reared, grinning fiendishly and snapping at the reins. The horseman gave a bow to heaven like a hanging man to his executioner and rolled from his saddle on to the ground. (From *Palace of the Peacock*, p. 19)

Donne is a conquistadorial horseman, the wild twin brother of the I-narrator who is nameless in the novel. Identity becomes a twinship in the terrifying, ecstatic life of the family of humanity to which we all belong, in which we are all reflected in the heights and in the depths of history. My grandmother on my mother's side was half-Arawak, half-European. The Arawaks were a gentle, very gifted people but they were called savages. My grandfather (my mother's father) was Scot and African. Such a family tree is not unusual in the South Americas. I perceive my antecedents within dimensions of dual and multiple theatre. In other words, even if they were not my biological folk – or if I were in pure (so to speak) lineal descent from one or the other ethnic ancestor – I would still claim them all within a descent of the imagination that links the animality of the painter Titian to the scored visage of a sculpted Benim priest or to a pre-Columbian Arawak/Carib infant riding a jaguar steed against the sun. Jaguars were children of the sun in ancient American legend.

Georgetown was known as the Garden City of South America in the 1920s. It was famous for its botanical gardens, its flowering, exotic trees, its elegant colonial houses not of stone or Grecian marble but of hardwoods and soft-woods transported down the Demerara and Essequebo Rivers to the low-lying coastlands from accessible forests beneath the rapids and waterfalls some sixty miles upriver from the sea.

There, at those rapids and waterfalls, the landscape began to change pro-foundly and dramatically. The land began to rise. The rivers were now above the reach of the Atlantic tides. I remember the great cathedral forests and how they rained gently at times with splintered leaves and sun. Parrots wheeled at sunrise and sunset above the wide rivers as if they were blind yet steady as a clock. I used to set my watch by them on expeditions into the heartland of the country.

The inaccessibility of the Guyana rainforests in the 1920s, 1930s, 1940s, 1950s – the difficulties exploitative agencies encountered – helped to stave off further decimation of the descendants of pre-Columbian peoples living there since the sixteenth century when the Spanish conquistadores Cortez and Pizarro penetrated Mexico and Peru. It helped also to protect invaluable flora and fauna, chattering creatures, and rare birds. I remember on my first expe-dition in the 1940s being greeted by the cry of the "who-you" bird as it was called by an old bushman in my party. WHO-YOU? WHO-YOU? WHO-YOU? As I listened and wondered how to respond, the interior seemed a million miles away from Georgetown.

And yet it was as if that cry had been heard on the coastlands. It was the theme of a ballad or calypso played by the tall stilted dancers who danced through the streets. The mimicry of birds by humans requires a far-reaching chapter in the psychology of music. Likewise the links between dance and architecture have not as far as I am aware been explored. Do dancers sus-ceptible to the tremor of earthquake regions follow in some degree, subcon-sciously, unconsciously, the rhythm of a vessel sliding on a wave? The tall dancers in the streets of the Garden City danced in midair with a slightly rolling motion as upon an invisible tide. Their lofty station – the elongation of their bodies into artificial stilts and legs – reflected the great skill of the dance. It was curious to see them – how their pillared being achieved a counterpoint to the equally pillared slender columns upon which the houses in the city stood and appeared to sail motionlessly, as it were, above the ground. For in point of fact the ground of the city was beneath sea level. The houses therefore were uplifted as a precaution against flood waters from ocean and river.

I remember how the dancers would bring their masked features close to windows and doors, proffer an agile fist or a begging-bowl, and appeal for a fee for their extraordinary performance.

I did not realize fully then – though I sensed it in the marrow of childhood – that the dancers were performing a parable of a flood. On the western boundary of the town lay the mile-wide estuary of the Demerara River against which earthen dams, in need of continuous repair, had been built. On the north, conjoint with the river's estuary, lay the Atlantic Ocean.

In the heavy rainy season the pressure on the dams became ominous when it was reinforced by high spring tides from the sea. The Dutch, who were colonial masters of the territory in the eighteenth century, had built a sea wall against the ocean. I remember walking upon this when the tide was low and the ocean glistened half a mile and more in the distance.

On the other side of the wall, as one moved east, were football, tennis and cricket pitches stretching to the edge of the residential areas.

A word now about the Demerara conservancy or reservoir on the south and the southeast of Georgetown. For this may help me to extend, I hope, the parable of the flood, of the vessel and cradle of revisionary resources that the complicated Guyanese landscape was and is for me as I retrace my steps into the past in this essay.

The conservancy had been designed in the nineteenth century by English engineers to supply the city and various settlements and sugar estates upriver and to the east with drinking water and irrigation water.

I became acquainted with it for the first time in 1932 or 1933 on a picnic with a couple of friends. It appealed to me as a benign, dark stretch of water that seemed to burn in the sun. Stately palm trees grew close to the empolder dams. There were one or two fishermen on the dams with outstretched rods. It was a scene that could have been painted by Constable. The conservancy reached for miles it seemed and occupied an apparently level expanse of partly wooded, partly savannah countryside submerged to create a reservoir.

It was not until the late 1940s that I learnt – as a member of a land surveying team carrying out a new penetrative reconnaissance of the Demerara catchment – of an oversight in the construction of the conservancy. Straight-lined dams with occasional changes of bearing and parallel works – laid out more or less with indifference to the subtle gradients of the topography and to the incremental buildup of contours higher up the river – constituted an economic model for the needs of industry in the *immediate locality.*

We are now coming abreast of the pollution of environments in the late twentieth century. But apart from this the object lesson of the conservancy for me was the mirror it held up to the life of great rivers – such as the Demerara, the Essequebo, the Berbice in the Guyanas – which have their rushing headwaters in untamed and peculiar regions. A frame of settlement and reservoir on the Atlantic coast – however remote it appears from such headwaters, however fortressed to serve its own ends – may become a trigger of environmental crisis within a system of intricate forces and dimensions extending into the body of a continent.

That continent may be despoiled. The dangers as our century draws to a close are manifest in Brazil and elsewhere. The consequences would be dire for humanity. Then the tyranny of immediate gratification or parochial blindness to the mysterious book of landscapes would have triumphed. It has not yet happened. There is still a chance. Landscape is not a passive creature. It is a series of revisionary texts within nature and psyche, the nature of psyche, the psyche of nature, revisionary insights into the problematic reality and spirit of the arts and the sciences. My experience in and perception of South America is such that I could never take these for granted whatever gloss or lustre or privileged status of persuasion was placed upon them.

In 1973 I was invited to speak at a conference at the University of Missouri–Kansas City, and I spoke there of a narrow escape from drowning I experienced twenty-five years earlier just after the end of the Second World War.

We were gauging the Potaro River for hydroelectric power and had chosen as our station a section where the river narrowed and then opened up again to run towards the

Tumatumari rapids a mile or so away. We set up a base line on one bank with alignment rods at right angles to this. We were thus able to align ourselves and anchor our boat in the river, one anchor at the stern and another at the bow. Then with a sextant we took a reading in order to calculate distances from the bank as we made our way across the river. The Potaro River is strangely beautiful and secretive.

When the river falls, the sand banks begin to appear. At the foot of the Tumatumari rapids or falls the sand is like gold. Above, an abrupt change of texture occurs – it is white as snow. When the river runs high the sand banks disappear. We were – on the particular expedition to which I am referring – gauging the river at a very high and dangerous stage. The water swirled, looked ugly, and suddenly one of the anchors gripped the bed of the stream. The boat started to swing around and to take water. We couldn't dislodge the anchor. I decided that the only thing we could do was to cut ourselves free. So we severed the anchor rope and that was the end of that. Two or three years later, gauging the river in the same way, the identical impasse happened.

Once again the anchor at the stern lodged in the bed of the stream. And this time it was much more crucial because the boat swung so suddenly, we took so much water, that it seemed to me at that moment that we were on the point of sinking. I am sure I could not have swum to the river bank if the boat had gone down because at that high stage I would have been pulled into the Tumatumari falls and decapitated by the rocks. As the boat swung I said to a man behind me: "Cut the rope." Well, he was so nervous that he took his prospecting knife and all he could do was a sort of feeble sawing upon the anchor rope as if he were paralysed by the whole thing, the river, the swirling canvas of the stream. And then another member – the outboard mechanic – gave a sudden tug and the anchor moved. The boat righted itself. Half-swamped as we were, we were able to start the outboard engine and drive towards the bank. We began pulling up the anchor as we moved in. We got to the bank and then were able to bring the anchor right up when we discovered that it had hooked into the one we had lost three years before. Both anchors had now come up.

It is almost impossible to describe the kind of energy that rushed out of that constellation of images. I felt as if a canvas around my head was crowded with phantoms and figures. I had forgotten some of my own antecedents – the Amerindian/Arawak ones – but now their faces were on the canvas. One could see them in the long march into the twentieth century out of the pre-Columbian mists of time. One could also sense the lost expeditions, the people who had gone down in these South American rivers. One could sense a whole range of things, all sorts of faces, all sorts of figures.

> There was a sudden eruption of consciousness, and what is fantastic is that it all came
> out of a constellation of two ordinary objects, two anchors. (From *Explorations,* pp.
> 59–60)

Is autobiography an art? I do not know. Does retracing one's steps imply
an oscillation? Does it imply a cyclical as well as a spiralling vision? Does it
imply a pendulum that moves from side to side as well as forwards and backwards within a clock and calendar of space? With the mysterious death by
drowning – if he did die by drowning – of my stepfather, my mother, my
half-sister, and I went to live with my grandfather. He was a retired civil servant. I idolized him. He seemed so secure, so wise, so strong, so kind. With
hindsight I think he would like me to accept the fact that he was a child (as
much as an old man is a child) of his century – more nineteenth than twentieth century – a child of the Garden City. He was approaching eighty when
we went to live with him in 1929. His wife – she was his third wife – was not
my grandmother. I never knew my grandmother but learnt she had died
when my mother – the last of four children – was born. There was no offspring of my grandfather's second marriage, and his third to a woman of his
own age did not occur until he was in his sixties and in retirement.

My cousins were all some fifteen years or so older than I. My mother,
Millicent Josephine, was younger than her brother, Edwin, and her sisters,
Beatrice and Lucilla. Lucilla died before I was born. Beatrice became the wife
of the distinguished politician and historian A.R.F. Webber.

My mother, unlike Edwin and Beatrice, married late. She was thirty-seven
when I was born. My father was in his middle fifties when he died.

The stay with my grandfather lasted close on eight years. He was immortal. His secure roof seemed paradise. I tried to banish the thought from my
mind that he would die. But when it happened in 1937 I was not stricken or
overwhelmed as I thought I would be. He had been ill for a year and I witnessed the crumbling of a monument then. He was vulnerable, he suffered.
And when he died I was astonished to experience something akin to relief. I
released him in my imagination from pain. He released me to live and
remember him for what he was, a mortal man. It was his blessing.

Dostoevsky is the genius of possessed character in the nineteenth-century European novel, possession that crumbles within the cul-de-sac of impe-

rial order. He has written somewhere (I think it is in *The Brothers Karamazov*), of a saint who dies and is expected by everyone to smell of roses. It does not happen. My interpretation is that the blessing one receives from the dead and from the complex life of spirit in nature is not in a perfume or in the conscription of a rose. My grandfather believed in the resurrection of the dead and I have wrestled with this theme in my novels. Wrestled with it through alterations in narrative shapes in which the eye of the mind recognizes what it thinks it knows or remembers, what it forgets, what it remembers in a new and original, revisionary light.

In an interview in August 1990 by the Scottish poet Alan Riach, I was questioned about this. And I approached the enigma of the resurrection of Christ by referring in the first place to Sophocles' *Antigone* in which the status of death is absolute. Hades triumphs. I referred to the action of blind fate superbly dramatized in the play, the blind seer Tiresias whose counsels about the sacred necessity to bury Antigone's brother, not to leave his corpse exposed on the street, fail to plant seeing eyes in the heart of Creon, king of Thebes. Tiresias's prophetic blindness which sees but fails to enlighten the king becomes a counterpoint to Creon's spiritual blindness of heart. Oedipus himself – Antigone's father and the father of her dead brother – was blind. The entire cast is submerged in a tragedy of restrictive vision. At the dawn of the Christian age we find that classical blindness inserted into the textuality of the Gospels. The resurrection therefore is not a rhetorical proposition. It takes up afresh the burden of classical tradition. The disciples and Mary Magdalene fail for some time to recognize or see the shape and features of the resurrected Christ.

Yet a change was occurring in the frame of classical tragedy. The absolute status of Hades, of death, was changing. The change occurs in the life of problematic texts, the mystery of language within which the dawn of a new age cannot be taken for granted for it brings veils which part and yet through which one sees with difficulty. The restrictive vision of the past cracks a little in a wholly new way. The narrative is suffused with new particularities that conceal at one stage what is before us. But we begin to recognize what at first is unrecognizable. We recognize the unrecognizable by plumbing, in some degree, new particularities inserted into the body of tradition. The link with the resurrection is born then, I would say, out of potential that has been bypassed or eclipsed within texts of classical order, a link that begins with uncertainty to break certain formal assumptions and to disclose a deeper originality or thread or continuity running out of the past into the present and the future.

My grandfather loved his small garden with its roses and sunflowers. He was the child of the aesthetics of the parochial Garden City. He was blind to the threat of endemic flood built into the settlements that surrounded him. Yet not entirely unseeing. We were all, in some degree, passive creatures and victims of habit. Now – so long after his death – I would inscribe upon his grave a new epitaph that may do justice to his faith in the resurrection. That epitaph would imply links between imageries, yet differentiation in imageries, to bring home a wholeness beyond immediate or partial grasp. A ROSE IS A PARTICLE IS A WAVE.

Queen's College in Georgetown was the premier educational institution for boys in the 1930s from preparatory school age, around nine or so, to matriculation or preliminary degree stage, seventeen or eighteen. I was a student there from 1934 to 1938. Fees were high and it was rather a strain on my mother, particularly after my grandfather's death. No statistics may explain the curious phenomenon Queen's College was, the voyage upon which it was embarked as a vessel of learning linking old worlds and new. It is easy, for instance, for me to quote from a dusty archive of memory and say I left at the end of 1938 with credit or distinction in English, Latin, history and mathematics. The last was not my favourite subject, but I could enjoy the elegance of geometric and algebraic proportions, and at a time – when unemployment was endemic in the colony – it became the basis upon which I was able to study the trigonometric properties of land surveying (astronomy, geomorphology, hydrography, engineering-surveying, topography, etc.) under government auspices as was the custom – though one could also prepare for the stringent territorial examination with a private tutor – in the British Empire in the 1930s and 1940s.

Later it became more prestigious for young men to study at a university abroad or at home. The University of Guyana was not founded until the late 1960s.

Having paid due regard, as it were, to archival statistics, I return to the peculiar – even somewhat precarious – microcosm Queen's was in the 1930s. It was never quite the same, I believe, after the Second World War with the eruption in its wake of fanatical racism and the ideological and implacable confrontations that were enshrined and embalmed between East and West in the late 1940s and the 1950s.

I retrace my steps into Queen's in my novel *Carnival* within the shadow of a boy called Everyman Masters, who is being educated to climb upon a mule or horse as a prince or overseer of the plantation world of the Guyanas. When he eventually leaves Queen's and becomes an overseer, he is mistakenly identified for a treacherous lover by a peasant woman of his estate, stabbed by her, drawn in anguish to experience his first metaphorical death – the woman's knife in his ribs – within a "twentieth-century divine comedy of existence".

Though the section in my fictionalization of Queen's is a limited area of the novel, the implications of linkages between dimensions of a twentieth-century *inferno, purgatorio, paradiso* are subtly there within a cradle of learning that involuntarily perhaps breaks a ghetto-fixation with an absolute *inferno* and an absolute *paradiso*.

Everyman Masters becomes a Virgilian guide after his second, real death in London, England, to which he emigrates from Guyana with his young friend Jonathan Weyl. He returns in Weyl's dreams. Let us remember that Dante's Virgil was forbidden entry into the *paradiso* because he had been born in a pre-Christian age and was therefore a pagan. This taboo or sanction of fate is fractured when Everyman Masters as a boy in 1931 enters Queen's through a gateway or door over which is inscribed:

THE AION IS A BOY WHO PLAYS
PLACING THE COUNTERS HERE AND THERE
TO A CHILD BELONGS THE COSMIC MASTERY

Who is that child? What cross-cultural medium or microcosm of universal being does he bear which is to exact a price upon him in an altered fabric or narrative of tradition with its linked dimensions of *inferno, purgatorio, paradiso?*

Long before the United States was to embark upon desegregation in its institutions of learning, no barriers existed in Queen's, in classrooms, upon playing fields, between students or masters of different ethnic background. There were English masters and students, there were masters and students of African descent, Asian descent, Portuguese, Chinese, Welsh, Scottish. There were students and masters of mixed descent.

The inscription above the gateway through which Everyman Masters passes in *Carnival* is attributed to Heracleitus the Obscure. It seems apt to me for a variety of reasons. Greek was still being taught at Queen's in 1931, though by 1934 when I became a student there it was no longer in the curriculum. Nevertheless, though we read Shakespeare, Donne, Milton, Pope, Coleridge, Tennyson, Wordsworth, we also read Latin texts, Ovid, Caesar, Sallust. But that was not all. In the college library I remember coming upon a slightly terrifying, gripping, marvellous picture of the sculpture of the birth of the maize god. An arm's length away was another volume with a photograph of the ceiling of the Sistine Chapel. True, I grant, the ceiling was painted a decade or so before the conquest of ancient Mexico and Renaissance Europe's encounter with the maize god. But many who were to worship there in succeeding decades and generations – including Michelangelo himself who died in the middle of the sixteenth century – were to experience a blossoming, a flowering of creation, a new genesis, when the food supply of sixteenth-century Europe was virtually doubled (according to the American historian George Vaillant) in the wake of the conquest of the ancient American cultures and civilizations.

There was something prophetic, I am inclined to say, in Michelangelo's intuitive choice of genesis, of creation themes, in his great paintings upon the ceiling of the Sistine Chapel. These are I think a symbolic inscription, a wonderful gesture pointing backwards into Biblical legend, forwards into the New World. Indeed Columbus had already sailed upon what is now known as the Caribbean Sea, but the conquistadores Cortez and Pizarro had not yet encountered the god of maize and his irrigation systems of genius that sustained a variety of fruit, vegetables, potatoes, tomatoes, all exciting and unknown to Europe at that time. The birth of the maize god portrays the labour of the creaturely sculpted woman from whose body we see an infant child emerge. A curious counterpoint to the fatherhood of the universe painted by Michelangelo, but a valid and creative one it has taken centuries for our civilization to take on board on the male-dominated ship of the globe.

Queen's College did not have actual courses that dealt with the Americas as a whole but there was no overt censorship of books in the college library nor in the public library in Main Street – a stone's throw from the Catholic school I attended at the age of five – endowed by Carnegie.

My curiosity was aroused as never before during those years at Queen's. I grew aware of ambiguities and questions I could barely frame to myself in the 1930s, questions that were to haunt me in the years that followed. Questions that are at the root of novels I did not yet dream I would write, though their shadow may have been there (who knows) for I have not forgotten – it was sealed into my mind, a wondrous compliment and prophecy one cherished – an occasion when my English master said to me when he had read a story-essay I had written, "One day, Harris, you will be a novelist." I could not believe my ears and floated for the rest of the day in space. I remember certain things about him vividly. He was scrupulously fair in marking papers and had no favourites which made his remark all the more telling. He smoked hard – pipe and cigar – I could smell the strong tobacco on his breath when close to him. His skin was very pale, hair black as coal. He tended sometimes to come into the classroom unshaven but extraordinarily alert and sensitive to the needs of the students.

There was an irony, a humour, about his approach to books. He would comment wryly on the nature of censorship, the way censors could promote bestsellers. For instance forbidden books! Have them on your drawing room bookshelf, read or unread, at any price. It was the surest way to impress your friends at a Sunday morning cocktail party. He had sought out Aldous Huxley's *Brave New World* in the first place because of a rumour that it had been banned in Australia though no one had the slightest notion why. He had lost his copy and asked us – the students – whether any of us had seen one around. He had been unable to obtain it in the public library.

Forbidden books were good business. They were projected around the globe by way of rumour and legend. Books were intricate and complex commodities and sometimes works of genius fell to the bottom of the pile, lost, forgotten, and yet they returned and survived against the greatest odds. The funny thing is that I knew he meant it, that despite his wry humour he was serious about the life of the imagination.

I formed the impression that this master was not popular with his colleagues and that he resigned or was sent packing.

In *Carnival* I fictionalized him into the character Delph: *not* by any means an identical portrait. Nevertheless, there is a correspondence that is drawn from his inspirational practice in the classroom. He used to ask us to write narrative that incorporated various motifs or symbols or objects he would list on a blackboard. He was the most imaginative English teacher I had at Queen's, and his transposition into Delph – half-human, half-oracle – is set out at one stage in *Carnival* in the following passage:

> In 1931, as if he anticipated the sack, Mr Delph gave Masters several As for English composition. His habit was to inscribe a list on the blackboard and to request his students to incorporate it into a story. One such prophetic list, straight from the oracle's blackboard mouth . . . ran as follows: marble woman, burning schooner, crocodile, milk, Magna Carta, Bartleby's widow. (From *Carnival,* p. 75)

The resources of "divine comedy" in our age may lie, I feel, in the way we relate the ancient to the modern to illumine the enigma of prophecy that teases the imagination in Delph's list. The founding of a colony in the ancient Greek world was a sacred matter. Take the crocodile. Ponder on the peculiarity of its eyes. The Delphic imagination may lift those eyes from the margins of the world – from what nowadays we would call a mere colony – into the milky way. The crocodile's eyes, hidden in the darkness of a creek at night, glow astonishingly when they are addressed by a pencil of light issuing from a torch in one's hand. They become stars in an underworld sky. They witness to a link between creature and constellation. Such linkages – as in Quetzalcoatl, the god-man of ancient America who is flanked by coatl, the snake, symbolizing the earth, and quetzal, the bird, symbolizing the heavens or the sky – are native to Amerindian myth and legend.

Such linkages are inscribed as well in the constellations of the scorpion, the bear, the dog, the horse, the wolf. It is as if, I suspect, there is a therapy in such creativity, a numinous inoculation of the body of the mind which may heal us of dread forces or implacable animality within ourselves.

I return to the inscription above the gateway in my fictionalization of Queen's College: *The Aion Is a Boy Who Plays / Placing the Counters Here and There / To a Child Belongs the Cosmic Mastery.*

Perhaps the ancient author of that inscription possessed his blackboard on which he chalked a variety of counters to be moved here and there. Perhaps he was involved in a dimension of oracle in which an equation exists between a child's cradle and the birth of language. In every culture around the globe that equation exists in diverse and sometimes not easily recognizable forms. Hermes speaks to his brother Apollo on the day he was born. Or is there a tongue in the wood of the cradle? Does the rhythm of the tides in our blood infuse the vibration of the harp in the skeleton-tree in our flesh? Does the whisper of a leaf spell out the astronomy of dust? Every ventriloquist of spirit becomes in turn the instrument of what he mimics to break the mould of purely human pride or purely human discourse.

In the 1930s, it seems to me, curiously marginal or colonial institutions (such as Queen's College) in empires that were to crumble after the Second World War were aligned to unconscious/subconscious oracle. Guyana itself was a paradox. A doomed plantation economy yet one of the legendary sites of El Dorado. It was to experience decades later a vestigial dimension of holocaust in the sinister Jonestown massacre triggered by a group of American cultists during the Forbes Burnham regime when Guyana had become a republic.

The Jonestown disaster was headlined around the world in newspapers and magazines though it happened in a remote forest. One wonders in 1992 – the quincentennial year of Columbus's voyage into the New World – whether the enslavement of the Amerindians by the conquistadores who came in the wake of Columbus will receive the analysis it deserves in the world's press. The malaise of El Dorado is sometimes bleakly visible at the extremities of a civilization: the malaise of paradise, the malaise of gold. . . . Perhaps this is inevitable. The centres of a civilization are linked to extremity, extreme hope, extreme crisis. How can they evade, or escape from, dilemmas they have themselves helped to fashion across generations and centuries? Dilemmas, yes, but resources as well at the heart of history for revisionary momentum within an inner/outer voyage of the imagination . . . .

My own voyage outwards was consistent, I am sure, with my expeditions over many years along the coastlands and into the interior of Guyana. A landscape – a theatre of psyche and nature – I was to return to again and again in my dreams. I emigrated to the United Kingdom in 1959. There was an inevitability about this. The voyage out, the sense of the action of memory across distances, the sense of non-locality (or intense spatiality with its roots everywhere), had become an asset in unravelling restrictive orders or blindnesses. An asset and a key into the dimensionality I sought in the fiction I was beginning to write.

"Inevitability" – to which I referred a moment ago – implies a spectre of inner/outer consistency or necessity that may shape one's birth, the strangers one encounters at the gate of self. The Indians in India would call it karma. I prefer "freedom" one scarcely understands since "fate" and "freedom" are twins and can change one into the other.

My first marriage had ended in divorce. My ex-wife remarried and we remained on good terms until her death in 1964. I remarried in England in 1959. I met my second wife for the first time in 1954. I never dreamt we would see each other again. It was my good fortune that we did. Without her help over difficult times in the 1960s and 1970s, I do not think I would have survived as an imaginative writer into the 1980s. I owe much to her love and comprehension, and it was as if our relationship had been shaped by forces deeper than ourselves.

It was her second marriage as well. She was born in Edinburgh, Scotland, and had left in the 1940s to work in London. Hers was a singularly independent mind. In the winter of 1962 she collaborated with a young American composer as librettist in a television opera based on Charles Dickens's *A Christmas Carol.* Her libretto was highly praised by critics. She has had ten radio plays produced by the BBC. She is also in my view a fine poet.

We secured a flat in the Holland Park area in 1959. I had never been into the park or grounds of Holland House and was to have what I may only describe as a psychical experience there. My wife Margaret and I entered from Holland Park Road. We ascended a gentle incline which brought us to the edge of a pond. I stopped with a sudden, utterly startling impression. It was as if a host of persons unseen yet real came out of the trees calling, "Come in, come in, you are welcome here." I was taken aback, astonished. The impression was concrete though no one was in sight. Not a sound. And yet I heard voices of silence clearer and deeper than sound. They passed and I told my wife. The happening drove us to do some research about Holland House in the Kensington Library. We discovered that it had been the home of a famous English family who were renowned for their hospitality to writers, thinkers, poets and politicians. Had I been privileged to hear an echo of that hospitality? I was never to have that experience again though Holland Park became a favourite retreat of ours in the heart of the city. I listened many times but never again did the host of place, the voice or voices inscribed into place, speak. One welcome, one invitation, was enough perhaps and indeed I never felt less than welcome in the beautiful grounds surrounding the ruins of old Holland House bombed during the Second World War and converted later into a student hostel and an open-air theatre.

In 1977 my novel *Da Silva da Silva's Cultivated Wilderness* – which has a setting in Holland Park – appeared. In the passage I shall now quote, the painter da Silva writes to his wife Jen who is away visiting her sick father in Peru:

Today's one of those rare days that are so marvellous. I wish you were with me. Quite flawless, the light. What light. Subtle, translucent waterfall. No, tide, an ebbing and a flowing. Sun glints on leaves. Wind appears to stream through them until one catches a glimpse, the wind I mean, it's liquid. I would give my right arm to paint such light, the essence of unselfconsciousness . . . The weather's so lovely I've taken my easel . . . I think of you and hope the ordeal of your father's illness will soon pass. I entered the Park from Abbotsbury Road, ascended the avenue of limes to the statue of Lord Holland with the pond at his back. Paused for a while to make a sketch of green-headed ducks. The place is unique. Oaks, birches, chestnuts, cedars. Priceless woodland. And through a crack in the painted wood on my canvas I see peacocks and cranes. Took the paved path through rose bushes lit like lamps, curled flame, then across the stretch of green with its gnarled sentinel tree, down into the old Dutch Garden and on to the fountain under the clock. Fish in the pond there were darting gold, red, silver. A sudden bird flew through the fountain with a human voice, wing touching water, floating voice, sprinkle, close as the rooted hair on one's hand. (From *Da Silva da Silva's Cultivated Wilderness*, p. 27)

Da Silva da Silva was an acknowledgement on my part of the hospitality that the host of place – the invisible host – had bestowed upon Margaret and me within the grounds of old Holland House. The book did not sell well. And yet something odd occurred ten years later. Channel 4 of Independent Television set out to make a film on my work in 1987. Colin Nutley, the director, chose to base it on *Da Silva da Silva's Cultivated Wilderness*. I grant that within the limited budget at his command, it would have been impractical for him to take a crew into the landscapes of South America to film – let us say – *The Guyana Quartet*. Yet it gave me a strange feeling to find myself (I made two or three fleeting appearances in the film) standing in the eye of the camera close to the pond where Margaret and I had stood in 1959 and I had heard the echo of a vanished age and felt the warmth and the embrace of living absence or invisible presence.

I was to take occasional critics and scholars who came to see me into the grounds or park. There were excellent seats close to the old Dutch Garden and within tree-lined avenues. I remember taking Hena Maes-Jelinek there in the 1970s. Hena's background is European Jewry. She is a brilliant and unusual critic. She lives with her Belgian husband Rene in Liege and is professor of Commonwealth and English literature at the university there. Her interest in my work has continued across the years and is profound. She edited a remarkable book of essays by generous critics, scholars, poets – entitled *Wilson Harris: The Uncompromising Imagination* – that was presented to me (it came as a total surprise, even my wife kept the secret) in Paris on my seventieth birthday in March 1991. I must confess I was pleased by the diversity of contribution from writers such as Margaret Harris, Kathleen Raine, David Dabydeen, Michael Thorpe, Fred d'Aguiar, Kirsten Holst Peterson, Anna Rutherford, Michael Gilkes, Michel Fabre, Mark Williams, Alan Riach, Gareth Griffiths, Stephen Slemon, Joyce Sparer Adler, Russell

McDougall, Gregory Shaw, Nathaniel Mackey, Helen Tiffin, Louis James, Mark McWatt, Mary Lou Emery, William J. Howard, Al Creighton, Desmond Hamlet, Jean-Pierre Durix, Michel N. Jagessar and Hena Maes-Jelinek.

On certain occasions, not often, I have tended to discuss with Hena the haunting reality of the mystery of evil. She lost close relatives and friends in the holocaust. This is so unbearable that the imagination (whether philosophical or creative – and the two are linked) is challenged to the core of its genesis, *unfinished* genesis, I believe. I – on my part – am aware of the numinous and hidden scars on the body of cultures in South and Central America and in the Caribbean. Our dialogue has been fruitful. It has helped in the creation of an understanding of cross-cultural parallels and the deep bearing these have in overcoming implacable opposition and divides within a tormented world.

In this autobiographical essay I have attempted, in some degree, to illumine some of the forces and currents that bear upon the gestation and birth of a personal vision. I stress personal for I embrace no dogma, I have no absolute theories.

I close this essay with an unforgettable experience of a trip Margaret and I made to Mexico. We were able to go there in 1972 when I was a visiting member of faculty at the University of Texas at Austin.

Black Marsden – a novel which has much of its setting in Edinburgh (my wife's birthplace) – had been published that very year. The visit to Mexico was to provide me with a curious sequel called *Companions of the Day and Night*. The title is drawn from motifs of the great calendar completed within Montezuma's reign – a decade or so before the Spanish Conquest. That a fiction set in a layer of Mexican landscape and tradition should prove a sequel to a work largely set in Scotland raises for me a personal and private sensation of cross-cultural links between Celtic numinous darkness and pre-Columbian–post-Columbian uncertainties in the soil and ethnicity of all immigrant peoples in the Americas across the centuries. Africans possibly before Columbus, certainly through the Middle Passage, Scots after Culloden, Irish at the time of the great famine, Poles, French, Jews, English fleeing to the New World from persecutions. . . . Indeed a trigger of memory in me was fired by faces of Mexicans I encountered, reticent, slightly withdrawn, mixed ancestries, all pigmentations: faces in one focus stoically Indian/Aztec/Toltec perhaps, in other foci resembling my own mixed relatives and friends in Guyana. I remembered my own daughter, Denise, of whom I am very fond. She has something of that expressive spirit of curiosity blended into restraint and solitude that I glimpsed in some of the passersby in the Avenida Juarez. (I see her now afresh in my mind's eye as I write. She lives in New York and visits Margaret and me in Essex virtually every year. She is writing a novel.)

As we moved through Mexico City – its marketplaces, its museums, its halls, its churches (it was close to Easter when Margaret and I were there) in which Christ and his disciples were carven and painted in the colour and shadow of stranger gods, stranger sacrifices – the past seemed subtly alive.

The very dust that swirled on the road out of Mexico City to ancient Teotihuacan (which means "the place where the gods are made") seemed a sprinkling, a powdering, of a vanished reappearing dimension of fossil light. We passed convents on the way, ruins, the mouth of a tunnel into a mound or hill upon which a Catholic church stood. That tunnel led to a hidden Toltec shrine that had nestled in the earth for four-and-a-half centuries in concealment from the eyes of the conquistadores and their descendants.

We came around noon to Teotihuacan. We had read about it and knew it had been abandoned by its inhabitants – because perhaps of famine or crisis or some other circumstance unrecorded in the history books – long before the Aztecs arrived two or three centuries before Cortez. They named it Teotihuacan for they did not know its original name.

We set out to ascend the pyramids of the sun and the moon after exploring ruined shelters and palaces and corridors inscribed in places, it seemed to us, with child deities in swaddling clothes. Some had the head of young lions and birds. And there was a profusion of butterflies.

When we gained the height of the moon it seemed to us that if we gazed hard enough into a faint cloud of dust we would see the pointillist swaddling clothes – uplifted from the paintings beneath the pyramids of the sun and the moon – and this would tell of infant astronauts and the astronomy of long-vanished yet subtly alive poets and painters and sculptors and priests in space and in the memory of time. The light of the mind was their epitaph and our cradle.

Bibliography

Novels

Palace of the Peacock, London: Faber and Faber, 1960, reissued as Book I of the *Guyana Quartet,* London: Faber and Faber, 1985.

The Far Journey of Oudin, London: Faber and Faber, 1961, reissued as Book II of the *Guyana Quartet,* London: Faber and Faber, 1985.

The Whole Armour, London: Faber and Faber, 1962, reissued as Book III of the *Guyana Quartet,* London: Faber and Faber, 1985.

The Secret Ladder, London: Faber and Faber, 1963, reissued as Book IV of the *Guyana Quartet,* London: Faber and Faber, 1985.

Heartland, London: Faber and Faber, 1964.

The Eye of the Scarecrow, London: Faber and Faber, 1965.

The Waiting Room, London: Faber and Faber, 1967.

Tumatumari, London: Faber and Faber, 1968.

Ascent to Omai, London: Faber and Faber, 1970.

Black Marsden: A Tabula Rasa Comedy, London: Faber and Faber, 1972.

Companions of the Day and Night, London: Faber and Faber, 1975.

Da Silva da Silva's Cultivated Wilderness [and] Genesis of the Clowns, London: Faber and Faber, 1977.

The Tree of the Sun, London: Faber and Faber, 1978.

The Angel at the Gate, London: Faber and Faber, 1982.

Carnival (see below), London: Faber and Faber, 1985.

The Infinite Rehearsal (see below), London: Faber and Faber, 1987.

The Four Banks of the River of Space (see below), London: Faber and Faber, 1990.

Carnival Trilogy (includes *Carnival, The Infinite Rehearsal,* and *The Four Banks of the River of Space*), London: Faber and Faber, 1993.

Resurrection at Sorrow Hill, London: Faber and Faber, 1993.

Jonestown, London: Faber and Faber, 1996.

The Dark Jester, London: Faber and Faber, 2001.

Short Stories

The Sleepers of Roraima, London: Faber and Faber, 1970.

The Age of the Rainmakers, London: Faber and Faber, 1971.

Poetry

(Under pseudonym Kona Waruk) *Fetish,* privately printed, Georgetown, Guyana, 1951.

The Well and the Land, Georgetown: Magnet, 1952.

Eternity to Season, privately printed, 1954, revised edition, London: New Beacon Books, 1978.

Nonfiction

Tradition, The Writer and Society: Critical Essays, London: New Beacon Books, 1973.

Explorations: A Series of Talks and Articles, 1966–1981, edited by Hena Maes-Jelinek, Mundelstrup, Denmark: Dangaroo Press, 1981.

The Womb of Space: The Cross-Cultural Imagination, London: Greenwood, 1983.

The Radical Imagination, University of Liege, Belgium, 1992.

Selected Essays, London: Routledge, 1999.

Joyce Sparer Adler, 1915–1999

Joyce Sparer Adler is known worldwide as a brilliant scholar and critic in two areas of literary scholarship: studies of the novels and poetry of the nineteenth-century American author Herman Melville, and studies of the work of the contemporary Guyanese author Wilson Harris. Her essays on Melville's books, appearing at first as separate articles in journals, were later assembled in her book *War in Melville's Imagination*, and then were recast creatively in dramatic form in her book *Dramatization of Three Melville Novels: With an Introduction on Interpretation by Dramatization*. Her essays on Harris's books, also scattered in various journals, are now assembled for the first time in this volume. Before proceeding with a chronological outline of Joyce's life and work, I shall describe first how she came to have this special interest in the writings of Melville and Harris.

Her interest in Melville grew out of the graduate study she began as a doctoral candidate at Yeshiva University in New York. One of the books she read at that time was Melville's *Billy Budd*. The book impressed her as a powerful condemnation of war and its institutions. When she read what literary critics said about the book, she was astounded to find that they described it as "Melville's testament of acceptance", that is, as an expression of support for the status quo, including the articles of war which were the basis of Captain Vere's decision to hang the innocent Billy Budd. She resolved then to read all of Melville's writings to see what evidence could be found in them to support either point of view. When she found that antiwar sentiment permeated all of Melville's work she was inspired to write her book.

Her interest in Wilson Harris grew out of an accidental combination of circumstances. Joyce was a founding member of the faculty of the University of Guyana and taught there for five years. Those years included the period of "racial disturbances" when people of African descent were killing people of Indian descent and vice versa. It occurred to her that Guyanese literature, as a reflection of Guyanese society, might contribute to an understanding of what lay behind the racial conflict. She suggested to her colleagues on the faculty that someone should undertake a study of attitudes towards race in Guyanese literature. One colleague said to her, "Why don't *you* do it?" She responded that she thought it should be done by a Guyanese. This same colleague then sent a notice to a publication of the University of Puerto Rico saying that Joyce Sparer, a member of the faculty of the University of Guyana, is doing a study of attitudes towards race in Guyanese literature. When the notice was printed, he showed it to her and said, "Now you have to do it." And so she did. It was in the course of doing the necessary reading to be able to do this study that she first encountered the work of Wilson Harris and understood its importance. "Attitudes Towards Race in Guyanese Literature" was first published serially in the Guyanese paper the *Sunday Chronicle*. Then it was issued as a book by the University of Puerto Rico.

Joyce Sparer Adler (*née* Lifshutz) was born in Brooklyn, New York, on 2 December 1915. After attending New York public schools, she entered Brooklyn College at age sixteen and graduated in 1935 with the bachelor of arts degree *cum laude*. Later she did graduate work and earned a master of arts degree in 1951.

Her goal was to be an English teacher in the New York City public high schools. To acquire a licence as a teacher she had to take a highly competitive examination. (Hundreds usually took it, and only a handful would pass.) The bylaws of the Board of Education set the minimum age of candidates for this licence at twenty-one years. The board on some occasions would suspend the bylaws to permit highly qualified younger people to take the examination. Joyce knew nothing about such technicalities. She took the examination shortly before her twenty-first birthday and passed it. But since

The founding faculty of the University of Guyana

she was underage when she took the examination, she was denied the licence. Then, for a few years, the school board stopped giving examinations. When examinations were resumed, Joyce entered the competition again, and passed again. She taught in the public high schools from 1940 to 1954. During the last two of those years she was the acting chairperson of her department.

She resigned from her public school position in 1954 and then engaged in a variety of activities. She taught in three different private schools in succession. For two years she was editor of the medical journal *Blood*. During this period she also edited some medical books and a psychology encyclopaedia. She wrote a song that was among those Harry Belafonte sang for a Columbia Records recording. She wrote a play on school integration, "The Little Experiment at Jefferson Falls", which was bought by the Anti-Defamation League for television presentation nationwide, but it was never produced because of opposition from some of the league's southern chapters. Between 1954 and 1958 she taught English to members of some foreign delegations to the United Nations. In 1962 she was in a group of teachers invited to go to Guyana during the summer to conduct seminars for the teachers of that country at the teachers' training college in Georgetown. At the end of the summer she was invited by Premier Cheddi Jagan to return to help launch the University of Guyana. Thus it happened that she became a founding member of the faculty, and taught English there from 1963 to 1968. In 1938 she had married a fellow teacher, Max Sparer. The marriage ended in divorce in 1960. In 1968 she married the mathematician and author Irving Adler. She then resigned from her post in Guyana to live with her husband in Vermont.

Shortly after her arrival in Vermont she collaborated with her husband on the book *Language and Man,* published by the John Day Company in 1970. Then she turned her attention to her principal interests, the writings of Herman Melville and of Wilson Harris. She signed what she wrote as Joyce Sparer Adler so that readers would know that she was the same person who had previously written under the name Joyce Sparer. Her book *War in Melville's Imagination* was published by New York University Press in 1981. She became an active member of the Melville Society, and was elected its president for the year 1988. She was a trustee of the Vermont Academy of

Arts and Sciences from 1982 to 1994 and its secretary from 1984 to 1994. She was elected a fellow of the academy in 1989.

Her reviews of the books by Wilson Harris quickly established her reputation as a Harris scholar. As a result she was a featured speaker at the 1973 conference on Chinua Achebe and Wilson Harris organized by the University of Missouri, and at the 1974 International Conference on Commonwealth Literature in Liege, Belgium. In 1984 she and her husband went on a round-the-world lecture tour with talks at universities in Australia, New Zealand, Japan, China, Hong Kong, Singapore, Malaysia and India.

In 1989 the Berkshire Opera Company decided that they wanted to produce an opera based on a novel by Herman Melville. They asked Joyce to write a libretto for *Benito Cereno*. She wrote the libretto, but the opera never materialized because the composer who was to write the music did not get the grant for which he had applied to sustain him while he worked. Having done one dramatization of a Melville novel, Joyce went on to write two more, one based on *Moby-Dick* and the other based on *Billy Budd*. These were published together in her 1992 book, *Dramatization of Three Melville Novels: With an Introduction on Interpretation by Dramatization*. One of them, entitled *Melville, Billy and Mars*, was produced at the University of Kansas in 1995. In June 2003 there was a reading of her dramatization of *Moby-Dick* at the meeting of the Melville Society in Hawaii.

Joyce's last major literary project was her work as guest editor of the 1997 issue of the *Review of Contemporary Fiction* devoted to the work of Wilson Harris. While she was proofreading the galleys for this issue she discovered that her eyesight was failing. Her failing eyesight resulted in a series of falls that caused multiple bone fractures. On 1 September 1999 she fractured her hip and was taken to the hospital for surgery. She died in the hospital on 13 September.

Joyce Sparer Adler is listed in *Who's Who of American Women, 1983–1984* and in *Who's Who in the World, 1984–1985*.

Acknowledgements

The autobiographical sketch of Wilson Harris was written for Gale Research Inc. and appeared in the Contemporary Authors Autobiography Series, volume 16, published by the Gale Group. It is reproduced here with the permission of Wilson Harris and the Gale Group.

Chapter 1, "Wilson Harris: The Ideal of Unity", is an excerpt from "Attitudes Towards 'Race' in Guyanese Literature", published in *Caribbean Studies* 8, no. 2, (July 1968). It is reproduced here with the permission of *Caribbean Studies*. It was first published serially in the *Sunday Chronicle*.

Chapter 2, "The Art of Wilson Harris", was first published in *New Beacon Reviews*. Every reasonable attempt to reach this journal received no response, so it is reproduced here on my authority as sole heir and executor of the Joyce Adler estate.

Chapter 3, "*Tumatumari* and the Imagination of Wilson Harris", was first published in the *Journal of Commonwealth Literature,* no. 7 (July 1969), and is reproduced here with the permission of the *Journal of Commonwealth Literature.*

Chapter 4, "Wilson Harris and Twentieth-Century Man", was originally published in *New Letters* 40, no. 1 (Autumn 1973). It is reprinted here with the permission of *New Letters* and the curators of the University of Missouri–Kansas City.

Chapter 5, "Melville and Harris: Poetic Imaginations Related in Their Response to the Modern World", was first published by Didier in *Common-*

wealth Literature and the Modern World (1975). Didier has since suspended publication. The essay is reproduced here on my authority as sole heir and executor of the Joyce Adler estate.

Chapter 6, "Wilson Harris's *The Womb of Space: The Cross-Cultural Imagination*", was first published in *Kunapipi* 6 (1984) and chapter 7, "The Evolution of Female Figures and Imagery in Wilson Harris's Novels", was first published in *Hambone,* no. 6 (1986). Both journals have suspended publication. These essays, too, are reproduced here on my authority as sole heir and executor of the Joyce Adler estate.

Chapter 8, "Wilson Harris's Cross-Cultural Dialogue with Melville", is published here for the first time. The text is from a talk given at the conference on Canon Formation of the American Literature Association, May 1992.

Chapter 9, "Wilson Harris: An Introduction", was written for the *Review of Contemporary Fiction* (Summer 1997), and is reproduced here with the permission of Dalkey Archive Press.

The original manuscript for this book consisted of a typescript and photocopies of journal articles printed with different typefaces and page sizes. I am grateful to my daughter Peggy Ann Adler who converted it into a readable text in a uniform format.

Chapter 1

Wilson Harris
The Ideal of Unity

It would be impossible to conceive of a writer more free of racial exclusiveness, and more dedicated to its reverse, than Wilson Harris. In his work there is no "we" and no "they". There are many themes in his novels, but the central and recurring one, the one that is interwoven with every other and into which all are resolved, is "unity" – unity as the basic necessity without which we cannot achieve full humanity. The intensity of Harris's ideal of unity reflects how far from it is the reality to which he responds. Each of the six novels expresses faith in the possibilities of man, however yet unrealized. But in the world of Wilson Harris "One" is fulfilled only in the "Other"; division among men must inevitably mean division within each one.

The novels are reputed to be forbiddingly difficult, demanding the greatest, most concentrated effort. But the right approach is not effort, but rather the most open receptiveness, going along with the current of the work, with each novel to illuminate the others, as well as each part of any novel to throw light backward and forward on any other part – and then taking the voyage again, a new and richer one each time. There is pleasure and beauty from the start, but a Harris novel, like fine music, cannot all be taken in at any one time. For Harris, an original genius, must continually forge his own method to unfold his own vision of life, and it takes time to catch on to his new use of language, new symbols, new form.

Yet the novels are not so difficult as they are often said to be; nor are they out of this world, but very much of it. Their origin is in, and their significance is for, the concrete world, especially Guyana. They are about human involvement and responsibility, a common voyage on the river of time.

To express this, there are things which seem strange – at first. There are brothers, twins even, yet of different races. A character sometimes fuses into another, becomes another. The groups of people in the novels are made up of all "races" in Guyana and of characters who may be of any or all.

To communicate the sense of oneness, and to counteract the idea of uninvolvement, Harris's characters are created mainly from the inside. The reader does not often view a Harris character but looks out with him at the world, from within the other's consciousness.

In *Palace of the Peacock* the boat's crew at times living, at times dead, includes Portuguese, Indian, Negro, Amerindian and others. "The whole crew were one spiritual family living and dying together in a common grave out of which they had sprung again from the same soil and womb as it were."[1] They have been the pursuers of an Arawak group, at the behest of the boat's captain, Donne, who is a user of men, turning them to fit into "a compulsive design and blind engine of war" (p. 115). Then, themselves pursued, they sail beyond death. At first "it looked the most inextricable confusion to determine where they were and what they were, whether they had made any step whatever towards a better relationship – amongst themselves and within themselves – or whether it was all a fantastic chimera" (p. 84). Then all antagonisms clearly end.

It is true that unity is achieved in this novel only after death. But the implications of fable are for this world; as the narrator says, "Each of us now held at last in his arms what he had been forever seeking and what he had eternally possessed" (p. 117). The unity and the embraces have always been possible and could have been theirs without death.

In *The Far Journey of Oudin,* Oudin, dead, hears his wife and child wailing in the house. Ram, this novel's user of men, enters. The rest relates what led up to this moment. In that past Oudin comes, no one knows from where, to be made Ram's "slave" and instrument to be used against others. He arrives at a moment when three brothers – Mohammed, Hassan and Kaiser – have just killed their half-brother to whom their dying father wishes to leave land. Oudin resembles this half-brother whom another man, a black-skinned man, also once claimed as his own begotten son. The killing of the half-brother, perhaps descended from another race, starts the downfall and end of the family. They become vulnerable to the design of Ram who wants to seize all they have or produce. Brother after brother dies. Hassan is, I think reincarnated as Hindu, Kaiser as Negro. Mohammed, at the moment of death, fuses into the bull – the sacrificial bull; he trips on the trunk of a tree and falls and dies in the moment that he sees how Ram has used him too.

Ram wants Beti, daughter of the brothers' cousin, Rajab. He directs Oudin to abduct her for him, but Oudin feels a compassion that cancels out Ram's demand. He has at last a vision of freedom and he takes her away. They flee across pegasse, where one can dream, but nothing can grow. It becomes clear that Oudin *is* the murdered half-brother, robbed of his birthright and shunned "like one who had never been born."[2] He doubts himself – they would not have put themselves to such trouble for no reason. But he must affirm himself if he is to "rise above the grave of a world" (p. 217).

Beti too has always wanted to "redeem herself from being a kind of pawn" (p. 214). Her life has been filled with fear, but with the realization that she is to have Oudin's child, she has a glittering vision that "one faint day in the future all dreadful fear of life would vanish" (p. 230). For the first time she is able to make her own free choice, and she chooses that they return; she must save the unborn child. Still in their brief flight for freedom, they have planted this seed for the future and have prevented Ram from having an heir by Beti.

Then Ram sees himself: "such a fearful impotent man at heart . . . He lacked the grace and courage to plant a new seed himself . . . With the devil all things were possible, he knew, save the magic of potency and fertility and life" (p. 236). Yet he is not reconciled. To the end he plots to appropriate Oudin's offspring; but Beti, by a combination of instinct and a fleeting experience of freedom, frustrates this even after Oudin is dead, leaving another child inside her womb. In contrast with Oudin who has had no past, but who has planted a seed for the future, Ram has a past but will not have a share in the future; the enslaver is impotent when the slave refuses to be used.

The sources of violence and misery in this novel lie in the desire of some to appropriate the birthright of others and in the consent of those others to be robbed, murdered or used. Once the dispossessed refuse to be rammed into this relationship, the hope for the future belongs to them. That no one race is to be held responsible, but all, is made especially clear by the introduction into the novel of the story of a previous family in the area that had murdered an heir – a family of mixed Hindu, Moslem and African descent called the Allamans – all men!

The idea that the real identity of a Guyanese, of any origin, is to be found in Guyana itself and its particular history and not in the places that grandparents had to leave (Africa, India, China, Portugal) is the theme of *The Whole Armour* most relevant to this study. Harris sees the ancestry and identity of each Guyanese in all who have ever inhabited the land, even the "extinct" Carib. This theme and others weave in and out and interweave, coming together in an affirmation of belonging, not to any one group in the country but to the complete mixture of "every race under the sun".[3]

Christo is wanted by the police for the murder of a rival for Sharon whom he loves. (Christo's face is black, Sharon's white.) Actually it was not murder but accident, but everyone takes his guilt for granted, including Magda, his mother (a stunning literary creation whose words and figure almost leap out of the page), who is half Negro, half Chinese. She appeals to Abram to shelter him in the remote place where he lives, Jigsaw Bay:

> "But I want you to see, whether you eye blind or not, that Christo belongs to you as well as me. He could be your real son. I want you to forget yourself and feel this power of belonging. Is there anything stronger than mating and borning in this world until you lose your dying self? . . . Christo is you manchild by me. I make it so. I declare it so. Who in the world can say no to me? Am I not the best judge?"

"Don't be a fool," Abram protested harshly. "Christo is half me age, and is only yesterday I started sleeping with you . . ."

Magda suddenly burst into an electric laugh. "You is the biggest coward in the world, Abram," she said. "Even if you know me and had me wrapped in you arms a hundred lightning year ago you still wouldn't believe Christo is you flying seed and son; he too black and you too white." (pp. 247–48)

Abram takes Christo to Jigsaw Bay but he dies soon after, and Magda, who has loved him fiercely, is sure that Christo is guilty. She insists so impellingly that Christo confess, that he does, although again he is innocent. Magda puts Christo's clothes on Abram's body so that it will seem Christo is the one dead, and she makes him flee to Venezuela.

Weeks later Christo returns, after a wake has been held for him at which Sharon's new suitor, Matthias, has been killed by Peet, her father, in the same accidental way that her first suitor was killed, so that everyone, seeing the accident re-enacted, realizes Christo's innocence.

The police, however, are still coming for Christo, "still looking for somebody, anybody, upon whom they can properly and legally pin the blame for everything" (p. 327). But Christo has stopped running; he will never flee, as if guilty, again. He and Sharon, who has always believed him innocent, are on the gallery of her house, overlooking the river.

Sharon thinks of the people of the bush who for hundreds and thousands of years "had been labouring against the sun and the river, betraying each other and stabbin' each other, hounding their free spirit deeper into all of themselves". Christo's back that she caresses becomes one with the country. "Her fingers travelled across the map of Christo's skin, stroking the vein in every ancestor's body" (p. 308).

Matthias's father passes in a boat "staring stonily at the nervous conjunction of white and black face" (p. 332). He has always worshipped only his own son, as Magda has worshipped only Christo, and Peet only Sharon. Christo thinks of the parents of them all and makes the one long speech in the Harris novels, an artistic blemish that seems a sacrifice by Harris to the urgency of getting his convictions across without the time lag that would have to come before the public could grasp his usual, much more complex artistic mode of communication. (*The Whole Armour* was published in 1962, but written, of course, earlier.) The speech says they must face things before it is too late and plant in stable soil or everything will come tumbling down. Christo feels the parents are really the young people's problem children, all still Guyana's first aliens and arrivals, all looking backward, not ahead. He tells her what he thought he saw while on the run.

First he thought he was one of the fleeing tribe of Caribs. Then he was "every black ancestor and bloodless ghost. What had they done to be running like that, Sharon? What were they guilty of? I was one of them . . . one of a crowd of fictions. I was dreaming. No, God knows, I was never so wide awake . . . Then I said – look stranger, suppose this is South America where you belong?" (p. 343). He speaks of her father, who chased him when he first came to see her, as the last of the band hounding him on; of himself as the last member of the flying band. The child he and Sharon have conceived will not run. And a year later, "The child was crowing to the clock at five minutes to ten on the morning of the execution" (p. 347). The river in Harris's world flows on. The concept of continuity, of progress, goes along with belief in people and in the possibility of unity.

So concerned is Harris, in this novel, with rapid communication of his convictions that he conveys them with a rare explicitness: they are *all* our children; they must be freed of a feeling of guilt that has been inflicted on them for no good reason; running away from problems must end before it is too late; the soil in which everything grows must be stable not pegasse; now is the time to make a new stand for the idea that each man in the land will remain a stranger from the next and from himself until he finds his identity, not in the old countries and continents but in Guyana where he belongs.

How does a concern about the history and fate of a particular group in Guyana fit into the larger belief, expressed by Harris in *The Whole Armour,* that all Guyanese have their real historical past, their real identity, right here on the South American continent and not in Africa, Europe or Asia?

Harris does not spell out an answer to this, but *The Secret Ladder* holds some implied answers: the development of the group cannot be thought of apart from the development of the whole people; what the group must preserve and develop is its ancient spirit of freedom; they must not push this back into themselves by any unjust, violent act of their own – a form of self-repudiation. On the other hand the individual's conscience must not permit him to turn his back on the group he came from; he must associate himself with the most dispossessed and distressed of them. *The Secret Ladder* is "an inquiry into the dramatic role of conscience".[4]

Fenwick is a young surveyor whose mother is part English, part French, with an Arawak grandmother, and whose father was a "dark big man of vivid African ancestry" (p. 382). He meets the ancient Poseidon, leader of a group of Canje River bush Negroes who feel threatened by the survey Fenwick is in charge of. They are sure it is a prelude to an irrigation scheme that will flood the whole area and drive them off the land, taking their last freedom. Rumour has it that Poseidon's grandfather was a runaway African slave who evaded capture and became a wild man of the swamps. Now Poseidon is seen as "the black king of history" with "sovereignty over the past" (p. 369) and over the present too: "Old man Poseidon occupying here" (p. 368).

Fenwick's crew must gauge the river depths; Fenwick must gauge the depths of his conscience. There is something in his past he feels the encounter with Poseidon will make him have to face. It is "a question of going in unashamed to come out of the womb again" (p. 384). Poseidon, ragged and incoherent though he is, becomes for him the Grand Old Man of his father's history and his. At the same time Poseidon is like a fish he has caught, helpless and agitated, within whose aged body there is an ancient inarticulate spirit.

Fenwick's allegiance is divided when Poseidon's people begin to sabotage his measurements. But his allegiance to Poseidon is not a matter of shared race. "I owe allegiance to him because of his condition, allegiance of an important kind, that of conscience, of the rebirth of humanity. And that is the highest kind of allegiance of all" (p. 396).

The novel gives terrifying glimpses into the psychology of group violence. Chiung, a member of the survey crew, has almost been killed, though unintentionally, by two of Poseidon's followers. Weng, one of his superiors, demands that Chiung say some accusing words. "Even if you see nobody, just say you hate the body that strike you down" (p. 438). Chiung's refusal infuriates Weng. "You should be dead" (p. 439), he shouts. For if Chiung were dead, they would all go to avenge themselves on the tribe. But if there is anyone Chiung hates now, it is Weng, and he takes his stand against violence, "I refuse to be pushed around by Weng or anybody. Scorn me if you like, but don't push me into your design any more . . ." (p. 440).

In the other camp violence wells up too. Poseidon trips and dies. His followers, mad with grief, hold two of the outsiders, Bryant and Catalena, responsible. They abandon themselves to hate, "surrendering to the eternal . . . cage of themselves" (p. 457). They will punish the woman by rape, then kill both.

Bryant, who has loved Poseidon, seeks to protect the woman and himself; to keep the tribe from this horror is the last tribute he can pay to Poseidon's memory. So he "prayed and fought that they would reduce the sentence of self-repudiation they wished to pass" (p. 459) and *something* does in fact keep them from raping and killing until there is no time left for them to execute their purpose. "*At* the self-same moment that they were beginning to execute a picture of the void in themselves, their world was peopling itself afresh, against their will, against their bitter intention" (p. 462).

Poseidon's people leave the bush; it is the end of the tribe as a tribe. But Fenwick hears their voices echoing everywhere. "In our end . . . is our beginning." He awakens to the dawn of the "seventh day" (p. 464). Chaos has not come again. The world and humanity are born anew.

In *Heartland* the idea is put forward that a golden age of the past may never have existed; it is existence now that counts.[5] Identity is in one's time and place and in relationship with other men – seen or unseen, contemporary or of that past which is incorporated in the present. Closeness with other men because of shared feelings and experiences is conveyed in a passage in which Stevenson comes to a place in the forest that someone has passed, who has, like him, worked a random vein in the line. Stevenson feels "the cutting sensation of a presence so near him it lifted his heart like a fruit into his mouth" (p. 51).

When Stevenson comes to Kaieteur he sees it as the place where Guyana broke away from the South American continent, like the displacement of "river bed from river, watershed and island from the heart of a continent" (p. 70). This has caused too, a displacement of man in the wasteland separated from heartland.

Lost in the "directionless depths of the forest" (p. 31), he finds a place which the river (time and history) abandoned long ago before taking up its present channel. The ancient empty river bed is like a road, the road not taken. Stevenson takes it, turning away from the old ways that lead nowhere, "the self-created prison houses" (p. 90).

The novel's main theme is this exploration beyond the areas of settlement. But what is sought is still unity, in this case unity with the heart of the continent.

The Eye of the Scarecrow,[6] the last Harris book before 1968, is also the most difficult. The author places the reader almost in the role of psychoanalyst who must try to piece together "fragments of recollection", symbols and personal associations. In a way all of Harris's books are jigsaws; but the fact that in this book everything is in pieces holds particular meaning; for the narrator's mind is fragmented. A crash has shattered both his outer and inner world.

In this "novel" a new reading difficulty is introduced in the continual use of words with multiple meanings with all the meanings in play simultaneously, for example "depression" as economic, geographic, emotional and spiritual depression all at the same time. It is like seeing one photograph superimposed upon another, seeing each one and the combination of both at the same time (snapshots play a large part in this work), or like seeing an experience superimposed on the memory it arouses.

The reading is a "fantastic voyage" not, this time, inside the consciousness of the character, but his unconscious; and if the reader does not understand everything, neither is he expected to, but to keep searching. A great many insights come to the surface all along and are developed.

Written in 1965 the novel reflects the state of shock that has been the aftermath of events in Guyana that began in 1962: the riots, the killings, the destruction, the sharp division of the Guyanese people, the whole splitting of the "Guyanese personality". The lines of the poet Hart Crane, whom Harris quotes, speak of a broken world; Harris in *The Eye of the Scarecrow* speaks of a stunned one.

The book is in the form of letters and journal entries in the nine-month period from 25 December 1963 to 25 September 1964. They invoke memories so that they may reveal the seeds of a disaster, a "CRASH" that has occurred. Recollections of the depression years, 1929 to 1932, and of 1948, the year of the "Guiana Strike" and of the funeral of the shot-down demonstrators are evoked, with memory functioning in a strange way, for the writer's recent *stroke* has created a void in conventional memory.

The writer in London is writing to L. in Guyana, to whom he has been linked since boyhood, the one who has sent him snapshots (read newspaper photographs, possibly) of where the "reconnaissance machine" (p. 85) had crashed. The writer has been invalided out of the expedition. He is bewildered. "What was – or is – this crash one speaks of . . .?" (p. 100). The writer and L. are like and unlike, architect (envisioner) and engineer of the "framework of society" (p. 73). They are necessary to each other, yet they have had a violent quarrel before the crash. The writer needs L.'s help now, however, to find out the nature and cause of disaster. One view alone is incomplete, distorted.

His memory goes back to 1948, the "striking year" (p. 47) of the past, the year of the funeral procession for the shot-down strikers, the beginning of the swollen flood.

The growing flood image is a central one: the procession comes like a river of people pressing against the sea wall; the street they turn into is Water Street. Memory, also like a stream, flows back to 1929–32, when he was a boy living with his well-to-do grandfather in whose drawing room there is a painting of the Battle of Waterloo. (Water again, but now also a place of defeat.) And Waterloo is the name of the street in Georgetown where the grandfather's tenants live in a tenement range, in a long passage like "a frieze of subjective figures" (p. 30) with darkness at their back, "the subterranean anatomy of revolution" (p. 31). And the passages of memory are also subterranean.

By the time of the writing, the flood has swelled and the crash has come. The two who have quarrelled have been saved (someone else has died for them) and there is a moving towards dialogue; one cannot achieve recognition without the other, there must be a "transaction between TWO – one party to which is involved in the other's endless task of freedom" (p. 75). (In the light of events at the time of the writing of this book, the use of such words as "party", "crash", "quarrel" and "dialogue" is inevitably interesting, since the invocation of multiple meanings of words is such a conscious literary method throughout the book.) There is finally the idea that the crumbling of divisions separating people is the "secret of all creation" (p. 102).

The "novel" is obscure like the darkroom at the end where the final snapshot is developed. But it expresses with great clarity the staggering effects of the events of the 1960s in Guyana – though the seeds were earlier – that appear to the outer eye as simply a conflict of races.

But is this only a partial view? In *The Eye of the Scarecrow* the source of the shattering flood is the existence of an underground stream of under-privilege. And the united effort of the "One" and the "Other" remains the prime necessity in the endless task for freedom.

Harris's writing is like a valuable national resource. His highly original creative literary art has grown out of his most profound thinking, in the service of – and out of concern for – Guyana and the human race. As more people read the novels and the ideas radiate, they will have their effect on the consciousness of the Guyanese people.

Chapter 2

The Art of
Wilson Harris

I

Two new books by Wilson Harris were published in 1967: *Tradition, the Writer and Society: Critical Essays* and *The Waiting Room,* a work of fiction. They are interesting to consider in relation to each other.

The essays – articles and lectures written in the sixteen-year period 1951 to 1967 – put forward Harris's critical ideas with directness and clarity. It is not his style that is unconventional here but his outlook. A prefatory note by the author describes the series as "a groping towards something I could not hope to define except within a deepening cycle of exploration". The exploration, he emphasizes, is not to be considered as complete; to be complete is to be static.[1]

The same words, "a deepening cycle of exploration", well describe Harris's series of "novels" of which *The Waiting Room* is the latest, but certainly not the last; in Harris's imagination the exploration must continually be going on.

The style in *The Waiting Room,* however, is as indirect as the style in the essays is direct. Only readers who have followed along with him to this point in the deepening cycle of exploration in fiction will, I think, be able to find intelligible, at all, the personal and complex connotations that attach to words, images, symbols, shifts from one consciousness to another, and the ebb and flow of the imaginative processes in the minds of the "characters", as all these unfamiliar new methods of expression merge in the spiral-chambered form of *The Waiting Room*.

The interpretation of it which will appear in the second part of this review (and even this article on his critical theory) must emphatically also be understood to be only a "groping within a deepening cycle of exploration" of the world of Wilson Harris. Why, we inevitably ask, must a writer who can be so direct in essay form choose to write so differently in his works of fiction?

Harris's answers are to be found in his essays. To the imaginative writer art is not an appeal to intellect alone: it is, like life, the "sensuous phenomenon" (p. 7) meant to arouse the whole of man : intellect, all physical senses, emotions, energies, imagination, memory, critical evaluation of experience, creative power and hope for the future.

The artist has a responsibility to make a "contribution to an original conception of values" (p. 13). To arrive at values that are truly his, he has to first break out of the existing mould of frozen conventional preconceptions. And he must do this in a way that is disturbing, "so disturbing that vitality and power are realized as a strong possibility" (p. 15).

The disturbance is created by the purposeful juxtaposition of things opposed to each other. (The creating of the book, we might say, is the laboratory experiment intending to bring about, and to see what will come out of, the explosion that results when opposing forces are brought together.)

Only when conventional modes of thinking and conventional modes of language (the medium of thought) are exploded, will we burst out of the bonds within our own consciousness and, as a result, out of the bonds that oppress us in the exterior world. Then the inner and outer world will become integrated. At present they are at odds.

There is the "paradox of man's utilization of the energies of space and his oppression and unfulfilment". And "a gulf exists between the idealism of the world, its optimism and illusion, and the actual state of the world, its processes, its changes, its needs" (p. 7).

Man's fetishes need to be replaced by *human* values. "Man will never pass beyond prehistoric conditions until all his gods have failed, and their failure puts him on the rack, opens up the necessity for self-knowledge and for scientific understanding of his environment" (p. 17).

When the old rigid mould crumbles, the possibilities of the future are opened. When the toy-man, the exploited man, becomes aware of original rhythms within the oppression of his world, contradictions are bared in a manner terrifying and yet containing the secret of change (p. 19).

But to put this terrifying world in its proper relation, Harris tells us that "Man is frequently overwhelmed by the immense and alien power of the universe", but "within that immense and alien power, the frail heartbeat of man is the never-ending fact of creation". Self-knowledge by frail man will bestow "the authority he will bring into the rebuilding of civilization" (p. 20).

What Harris stresses for writers is the insufficiency of art that has as its theme only the "absurd" (p. 26) present. A unity must be established of present, past and future if the present is to give birth to a new whole human person able to live in community, replacing the "broken" (p. 27). isolated individual of today. Without the ability to break out of the isolation and to form community, without relationship, man is without reality; he is the toy-man of the present, an age of a "terrifying cleavage in the psyche of man . . . upon the brink of a great change or equally great disaster" (p. 57).

Fiction must explore the divided personality of man and investigate the contradiction that has developed between "the man who built a world and the world he built which made him helpless" (p. 19). Because of the connection between the need for knowledge of the outer world and for self-knowledge, Harris finds that two notable attempts to bridge the gap between man and the world he built, namely Marxism and existentialism, are "in the final analysis concerned with the same thing, though the identity slips constantly from our grasp" (p. 8).

Art needs to deal with these philosophical questions, but surely not in the form of philosophical treatise. So Wilson Harris recalls with interest Eliot's words on Dante, that he "more than any other poet has succeeded in dealing with his philosophy, not as a theory but in terms of something perceived" (p. 36). (What is often called the artist's vision is actually nothing mystical but a "visualization", or whatever word our language lacks, to imply intense perception by all the physical senses and the "realization" of ideas in terms of things perceived.)

Wilson Harris's art gives visual or sensuous reality to his ideas of the inner drama of man and of the world he inhabits. He finds that what his own experimental exploration demands is a "slow unravelling of obscurity – revelation or illumination within oneself" (p. 52), leading to revelation of our "peculiar membership one of another . . . the life of consciousness in a circuit of relationships" (p. 53). And since our awareness is not made up of "solo" sense impressions but of orchestrated sensations and responses, the art of fiction, to express reality, must present "convolutions" of images. "To prize these images apart is . . . to lose the dialectical field in which they stand or move" (p. 55).

Obviously this is not an easy kind of art in which to pioneer. It is almost entirely a new art, and experiment in it may, until its effects are felt, limit Harris for a long time to being mainly a writer's writer. But he feels that there is a tradition for his kind of art that is hinted at in works like Frances Yates's study of the art of memory – a forgotten art, an inner art – that she feels encourages "the use of imagination as a duty", and that must surely have been a major factor in the evocation of such amazingly new, and lasting, images as the grotesque figures in medieval art, which she believes "were created by imaginations striving to find forms that would prove memorable" (pp. 55–56).

As for the language of memory and consciousness, Harris believes it must literally rediscover itself if we are to break out of the mould of misconceptions of the past and unload the burden of "sacred" usage. In the "heart of darkness of modern man . . . achievement of co-existence between the ideological camps and races of himself may be won only at the sacrifices of embedded and cherished areas of habit" (p. 63). And those cherished habits and prejudices are embedded in frozen uses of language.

Harris brings up for consideration certain African writers who have been described as doing violence to standard English sometimes as an intellectual pastime, since standard English remains in their countries mainly a political medium and language of the elite only and they are in rebellion against this. He then goes beyond this to discuss the more profoundly experimental writers whose breakthrough springs out of a desire to divest their art of every new or old kind of exclusive and one-sided consolidation. In this experimentation there may well be "intrusion of obscurity" (p. 66) but he feels these are "constructive . . . agents in a dismantling process"; this is fertile, a pre-condition for a new "architecture" of the world "not for one race of men but for all mankind together. Not simply for a glorious name or tradition in the historical sense but for an identity which is purposive and vital in a universal and manifestly human sense" (p. 9).

To him identity means identification with the whole of the human race, its whole past, present and future, or it means almost nothing at all. Any narrower "sense of identity" has to be a broken, one-sided thing, unable to "see" or "hear".

So the annihilation of barriers, divisions, prejudices and old "dumb" attempts at communication is needed for the conception of a future whole *human* person. (A breakthrough must come just as a "wall" must first have been broken before a child can be conceived. The comparison is suggested by the sensuous sexual imagery by means of which Harris presents his evolving philosophy in the eighty pages of *The Waiting Room.*)

Anyone who has read *Tradition, the Writer and Society,* but not *The Waiting Room,* may wonder at my choice of highlights in a collection that includes, among other things, an exciting lecture on "Tradition and the West Indian Novel", with its extended, pointed, but constructive criticism of other West Indian novelists: John Hearne, C.L.R. James, George Lamming and V.S. Naipaul among others. But my aim was a unification of those theories in the whole cycle of essays that illuminate why Wilson Harris has to write his kind of fiction and to focus attention on philosophical concepts that are "embodied" in *The Waiting Room.*

I have omitted discussion of some basic sections in "The Writer and Society", a lecture delivered in 1967 at the University of Edinburgh, because that essay, in particular, should be attentively read in its entirety and reread in detail, in conjunction with *The Waiting Room,* by anyone interested in "seeing" how "essay material" may be "transmuted" into fiction when the critical, philosophical ideas are filtered through the "alchemical imagination" of the poet's mind (p. 57).

II

The art of Wilson Harris is different in kind from the art of anybody else. And *The Waiting Room*[2] is different even from the earlier art of Wilson Harris. Insofar as his experimental work is concerned, it represents a breakthrough, a leap in artistic development. Many of his problems in regard to the integration of scientific mind and poetic imagination have here been solved.

The male and female figures in this "novel phenomenon" are not individuals in any sense, but pure symbols. They are intended, not as "characters", but as essences – of separate man and separate woman at first and ultimately of one masculine/feminine principle – the human principle essential to the creative imagination.

By means of imagery associated with the physical union of man and woman, Wilson Harris communicates the lovers' progress: from what appears a simple sexual association – compounded of attraction and hostility – to their quarrel and separation, to their simultaneous imaginative exploration years later in the mind and memory of each, and then to a climax of inner discoveries that enable each to enter the imagination and consciousness of the other.

The male and female figures have proliferating meanings until they come to stand for all so-called opposites that need each other for survival and creation – opposites that overlap, that together are embraced by the paradox of separateness and oneness: fundamental opposites like night and day, choice and "fate", dissolution and creation, diverse heritages from the past and hope of a united future, and so echoing on and on.

The central figures reflect also the specific contradictions of our own age, that area of overlap of past and future that we call the present even as it slips momently into the past. They appear as the "*dramatis personae* of the universe" in our space age that knows so much and yet so little – that does not know the meaning of its past, and, like Susan Forrestal in *The Waiting Room*, cannot predict whether the child in the womb will be monster or angel.

Susan is "blind" and has been for a long time. Her lover is, in a sense, "deaf" and as a result inarticulate. Each lacks an essential sense which only a fulfilling relationship with the other can restore. For rapprochement and new fruitful union each must first break out of his/her icy mould of frozen prejudices, out of blind and deaf isolation, the illusion of individuality. *He* must abandon his static notion of what freedom is, and *she* must break out of her stone house of material comfort only. (Her new husband seems to represent the technological and material values only, to which she has been wedded.)

Harris uses the word "solipsism" to indicate the reverse of the creative, dynamic relationship Susan and her lover really need. Solipsism is the belief that the self is the only existent thing, the only thing one can know. What Wilson Harris believes is the reverse: that *only in relationship* can one know oneself – "as she lay beneath him (or appeared to lie beneath him) in lightning upheaval and distress . . . he knew he was . . . in process of being informed by her about himself" (p. 39).

How each becomes better informed about himself/herself by contact with, and fuller consciousness of, the other is the "story line" of the "novel". When the lovers are first drawn back to each other in the waiting room of imagination, they sit apart, each reaching separately for a truer understanding of the past. But they shrink from the "operation" as it comes closer, from the cutting away of self and long-cherished concepts.

They move in a spiral of advances and retreats, fearful of the void that abandonment of old premises may bring. And indeed, "It was as if a subtle explosion – orgasm – had rent both the dark and light flesh of the waiting room and the flotsam and jetsam one endured became a tributary offering, spiritual reversal, main-stream whose course enveloped one in the very gulf of presence" (p. 26). The gulf does confront them; yet the obliteration of the "bubble of personality" (p. 26) is a necessity before a vortex of activity and creativity can be set up in the void.

Susan has to relinquish the idea that he had violated her, wanted to dominate her and be her sovereign "sun". And he has to give up the long-held idea that she had wanted to envelop and devour him. In she past he had heard in her only the siren song of the flesh which he felt would destroy him.

He had fled from her, as Ulysses fled from Circe. But now he sees Circe and Penelope as one. He begins to hear Susan's song differently, and it becomes the song of "immortal flesh and blood". His flesh "for the first incredible pointed time" (p. 54) begins to sing.

The Woman assumes at this point a new significance for him and the reader. She stands now for the *concrete,* the womb of all origins, of all art; and the lover's figure in relation to her becomes the writer's relation to the world. The connection between the writer's imagination and the concrete life that surrounds him is what is being explored: "Resonance . . . Bond . . . *Thing* . . . It was the only thread of ascent and descent into the hold of creation" (p. 52).

The conception by man and woman of a new, more *human* being is one which can mature only in a favourable climate. That the climax of the book occurs only in the last pages, with a sudden change of scene from a large city to a clearing in the jungle, in what is probably Guyana, indicates where Harris believes that climate *could* be. But there is no assurance that it *will* be; in the expedition an Amerindian guide has been smitten by a bushmaster: "The tooth of cayman alligator was placed on the wound. Nothing prevailed – neither civilization's first-aid chest nor mesmeric tooth of the wild . . . THE MAN DIED" (p. 25).

Something *new* must come into being for man to survive; the incapacity of technology alone to solve the problem is underscored by the death of Susan Forrestal and her husband in an explosion that wrecks their home. Only their logbook remains.

It is in the imagination of her lover that Susan now resides. And he appears to the reader clearly in his guise of the artist in whose imagination masculine/feminine, living/dead, subjective/objective are now incorporated. Now that he is released from the prison of his sole self, he is able to feel vicariously the pains the Amerindian guide had suffered and he is able to undertake to guard equally with himself the bereaved wife of the guide, in whom he sees Susan in a new guise. He is ready to descend into the underground part of the stream (of time, history), to navigate the "middle passage" and to explore the cleavages in the country and the possibilities of new creative union.

The basic shape in *The Waiting Room* is a spiral. There is the embracing spiral of space and time at whose centre is the heartbeat of man. The vortex, too, is not a surface eddy, but a spiral whirlpool: when Susan and her lover give up their old beliefs and a void is created, "The 'waiting room' – part-present, part-past, part-future, it seemed – was falling through the dust of space, axe of memory, chopping sea, flying chip of vessel . . . and one was drawn by the skin of the vortex into the other's rent and beauty of consciousness" (p. 54).

The spiral appears in "the echoing coil of 'herself' she drew like the snake of time in itself around him" (p. 52, Bk. 1). Later that coil is to be echoed in the image of the "armature of love" (p. 79) (coil of wire around iron core in a dynamo) and in the "bushmaster of space" (p. 79).

And the spiral shape appears again in the seashell image at the end, when the basic visual spiral imagery and the basic sound imagery of "echoes" are merged. The lover is to explore El Dorado where the melting-pot idea of the New World may yet be realized. Much will depend on him. He is now ready to descend, like Ulysses, into his underworld, the part of history that is buried, to get his bearings afresh.

Entering "subterranean cave of Susan" – the essence of Susan in a new guise again – he hears an ancient blast "able to reach him in an echo long muffled and nurtured and preserved (like the sound of the sea in a shell) . . . Ancient metamorphosis. Endless creation . . . species of fiction within whose mask of death one endured the essential phenomenon of crisis and translation." Within the radius of the delayed blast he feels himself "begin to relive – with new awareness – his descent through the door of the middle passage" (p. 79, Bk. 2). And he becomes integrated into the spiral continuum of man – space – time.

The "novel" seems to be Harris's voyage to find a unifying theory of life and the universe, a voyage in which his exploration parallels that of his "characters". But, as Susan's lover explains, "Appearances cannot be grasped in their entirety . . . isolate something in order to examine it properly, as one thinks, and one arrests or appears to arrest, a web of processes. . . . And one can never keep dead in step." It is, in other words, never possible to overtake "the swift runner of life" (p. 67, Bk. 2). What one observes and studies, in the very moment of observation become something else. This, perhaps, is the essence of the web of processes: "the indestructible evanescence of life". *The Waiting Room* is a place of blazing light and glowing blackness – merging in the "existential of the rainbow". But the most radiant thing about the "novel" (the light music that grows out of its initially maddening obscurity) is the incredible "at-onement" (except for a few passages) of the philosopher's ideas and the artist's imagination. The most concrete metaphor to express that unity of form and content can be taken from the book itself – the seashell at the end that contains the sound of the sea (possibly the one called the chambered nautilus – the room, the womb, the vessel, the sea all being suggested).

The book has a rhythm that is part of the "convolution" of imagery that "cannot be prised apart" (*Tradition, the Writer and Society*, p. 55). There is, in the convolution, a merging of seemingly contradictory sense impressions, like the "seeing" of an echo. Or, as an example of the fusion of the imagery, there is the overlapping of the lover's sensory responses: "He felt himself quiver like a bat's wing upon the sheer cliff – radar fantasy – and discovered a flowering plant lying crushed beneath him, blue petal, dark veins, spatula of mesmerism, the minute grasp of hand and fingers, intimate overwhelming design" (*The Waiting Room*, p. 29).

There are also "echoes" of images. There are, for example, all kinds of waves: waves of the sea, light waves, sound waves, waves of memory and feeling, waves of thought that ebb and flow. There are echoes from the author's prefatory note to the "novel" itself.

The "note" supposedly gives clues to the reading of the "novel", but it is only after the reader begins to *sense* the "novel" that the clues make any sense, and then the echoes reverberate back and forth in the book as a whole. The most expanding echoes, however, are those that the writer sets up in the imagination of the reader. That this should happen is, I think, Harris's main purpose.

Chapter 3

Tumatumari and the Imagination of Wilson Harris

Anyone interested in gaining insight into the nature and potentialities of imagination should look deeply into Wilson Harris's *Tumatumari*.[1] This eighth of Harris's extraordinary novels reveals his unusually original imagination at its present high state of development – a height to which it has evolved in the practice of the creative process he described theoretically in his lectures and essays.

It is a process in which the imagination plays a role that is "passive" as well as active, not imposing itself upon the material under scrutiny but immersing itself in it, freeing itself as completely as possible from its own preconceptions and limitations, and being itself continuously transformed in the experiment. The imagination is encouraged to respond readily to all that the material suggests, to engage in the freest association of ideas, words and images, until the underlying relationships and processes (and the necessary ways to express them) emerge to be more actively observed and organized.

The purpose of the immersion is to free the writer's imagination, as far as is humanly possible, from the settled ideas and responses imposed by the established institutions of an age, institutions which inevitably seek to consolidate and perpetuate themselves (seek to preserve themselves "inviolate") in opposition to the fundamental reality of all life and nature – change. It is implicit in *Tumatumari* that man, if he is to survive the imminent danger of self-annihilation, will have to free and transform his imagination so that it will be able to work in harmony with the fundamental laws of change and re-creation, rather than, catastrophically, to resist them.

Imagination is embodied in *Tumatumari* in the "heroine" Prudence, this novel's representative of Man. She is the "soul of man" awakening in a transitional age that may have already begun, feeling at last the need to develop and transform itself if the family of Man is to continue. To understand herself and her needs and desires, she reaches into memory, the well of the past. The search for the significance of the history of her own family, a middle-class "mixed" family in Guyana, leads to an exploration of twentieth-century civilization generally, as symbolized by the life of this single "civilized" family, and expands further into an exploration of the relationship between the twentieth century in Guyana (the land of Harris's birth and development) and other times and other places. Only in this broader search can Prudence find her own real identity, her identity with the whole human family, its evolutionary past, its complex present and its two possible futures, not yet determined in this "moment" of history. The implications of Prudence's search reach out without limit backward in time, outward without limit into space and inward from one horizon of imagination to the next.

The implication is that in *Tumatumari* Harris, too, set out to put the history of his own family and country together, and that out of the immersion of his imagination in this material, *Tumatumari,* with its constantly widening implications, developed. For to Harris, the story of Guyana and its different peoples is charged with the deepest meanings and the largest questions. Out of his continuously widening exploration as he created *Tumatumari* came the questions: Of what contradictory elements is the civilization of our age composed? Out of what womb did it come? Is it capable or incapable of giving birth in its turn? Is civilization now a totally barren thing truly lusting for self-destruction? If not, is it capable of a new kind of conception, a conception of something new, capable of surviving after its birth, not something born to die like Prudence's child, something that cannot live since it is no more than an extension of the primitive past and the still-primitive present? Will the breakdown of life in this century and the consequent sense of the imminence of danger give mankind the necessary humility to surrender long-cherished but long-outworn and now barren concepts and idolatries? Can so-called modern Man bear to face himself as still no more than primitive, living by primitive concepts, still offering living sacrifices to his gods, still sacrificing himself and others in the name of separate "incestuous" family or nation, tribe or race? Will it be possible, in the terms of the novel, for the early, still-primitive Prudence (caring only about her own family and its story) to be transformed into a new Prudence with a wider meaning to her name? Can the real welfare of "one's own" and that of others be seen convincingly as indivisible? Can concern for the individual family and concern for the whole human family be fused by imagination, giving birth to an entirely new conception – that of an integrated, unalienated, creative and truly human Man? And, to return to Guyana in a broader, non-national sense, does the Central and South American "new world", the melting pot of ancient and new, and of many races and cultures, have, perhaps, the best potential for being the crucible of change in the world today?

The interaction of this rich mass of questions and material with Harris's highly cultivated and informed twentieth-century mind and fluid imagination results in what is undoubtedly one of the most complex novels ever written. Reading and rereading *Tumatumari* is a gruelling as well as a rewarding experience; it is a rigorous challenge to the reading ability and imagination of the reader.

One sign of the complexity of *Tumatumari* is that, in comparison with it, Harris's previous novel, *The Waiting Room,* can be described as relatively straightforward! A few comparisons with the earlier novel may help to put *Tumatumari* in perspective (in so far as its "method" is concerned) before this discussion essays an outline of its "story".

In the earlier novel it was possible for the reader, once he saw the main thread, to follow it through the labyrinth of the book. But *Tumatumari* has innumerable intertwining threads, moving up and down as well as across; it is densely matted, very much like the mat of half-submerged vegetation which Prudence lifts out of the river at the beginning of the book. In its density and complexity it is a counterpart of the material under consideration, the complex fabric of twentieth-century civilization in which are caught up innumerable strands of the past, even the ancient past before man was man.

In *The Waiting Room* there are only two characters and their role is soon seen as symbolic and complementary; they represent all dynamic and fulfilling "opposites". But *Tumatumari* has a dozen characters, no two exactly complementary, or contrasting, or simply "individual" but all in *some* respect "equivalent" to each other, so that all their significances are interwoven, until finally all the other characters merge into Prudence as she takes on the significance of humanity as a whole, on the hairline of transition to a new age – whatever that age will prove to be. Incorporating them all, she may, like the phoenix, be capable of being reborn, because she becomes capable of entering into the others (of past and present) and of letting them enter into and become part of her.

Tumatumari is different from *The Waiting Room* also in its imagery. Whereas *The Waiting Room* was made up of a set of related images, *Tumatumari* contains a myriad of images which do not resemble each other – images deriving from physics and microphysics, mathematics, chemistry, anthropology, economics, genetics and the study of evolution, and much more: images which are only slowly seen as related or "equivalent" to others in *some* respect, and then only in a philosophical sense; these relationships are not "visualizable", as were the waves and echoes of *The Waiting Room,* but are extremely abstract, involving such concepts as "reciprocity" or "interpenetration" of elements. Only near the end of the novel (in the section on the Canje River area) are the abstract relationships envisioned in a stunning artistic synthesis of almost all the novel's themes and concepts to that point.

With *The Waiting Room* it is possible to speak of the basic shape of the novel, as epitomized by the spiral seashell near the end. *Tumatumari,* however, has rather a *shaping* than a shape, a continuous growth and retaking of shape much like the gestation and evolutionary processes taking place in the various wombs in the novel: the physical wombs, the womb of history, and the wall-less wombs of space and imagination. All the developments come to be seen as part of "chains" of development, one thing growing within and then out of another which then disintegrates and yet lives on in the new, part of a continuity of overlapping rings or clasps. For example, there is the section about the embryo in whose genes (themselves part of an unbroken genetic chain) are the markings inscribed by innumerable ancestors, including the animal ones – inscriptions which at the same time anticipate the possible future, so that, in a sense, past, present and future coexist in the fertilized egg.

Gestation and evolutionary processes take place also in history as it is viewed in *Tumatumari* and the images of wombs, gateways, doors, passages of entry and passages of exodus have many variations in the work. Guyana (in its larger geographical, not national, sense) is seen as being like the Mediterranean of the past, a gateway between the past and the future. The history of the country of Guyana (that was British Guiana), which has been one of *de facto* racial separation and discrimination, is also conceived of in these images. A political speaker in 1953 says of the immigration and employment policies, that they constitute a kind of pass system in which "we need an economic pass from the right cunt hole to get through the doors of industry" (p. 75). But the emphasis is not on the wombs and gates and doorways and passages as such; the main stress is on what is taking place within or though them.

This kind of conception of the world, with its emphasis on dynamic change and evolutionary processes, expresses Wilson Harris's pervading scientific view of all aspects of human life, biological, psychological and social. The result, in *Tumatumari,* is a rare synthesis of scientific outlook, philosophy and art. Harris seems to share the belief of the physicist Louis de Broglie, that modern scientific approaches have enormous philosophical implications, illuminating realities of all kinds.

The scientific view is not a separate or superimposed clement in the work of Wilson Harris. There is in *Tumatumari* a thorough "interpenetration" and interaction of the philosophical, scientific and artistic conceptions. This is one of the book's strengths, but it is at the same time one of the things that makes the reading so difficult. For example, because the content and form are so completely one, the development of *Tumatumari* is not novelistic or even literary in any usual sense, unless we are to conceive of the work as a long poem, which in a way it is. Its development is more musical than anything else: a prelude states the theme, but in disguise; then comes the appearance in a kind of hide-and-seek, of the various elements of the story that Prudence raises up from the well of memory; this is followed by the coming together of the significances of these memories and the emergence of the underlying themes and rhythms, which brings the work to a climax; then in the last section there is a restatement on a new level of the question implied in the prelude, and the work closes with a series of chords that are left suspended, suggesting a further development in the silence that follows. Eventually the reader who has come so far returns to the prelude which is now seen not only as an introduction to the work but as a kind of allegorical summary of it. Until this process of the development of the novel is perceived, the difficulties of following the "story" are great.

The story itself is so many-faceted that it is possible to suggest it only in rough outline. In what can be called the prelude, or overture, Prudence comes down to the river from her house on the hill at Tumatumari, which is deep in the interior of Guyana. The time is just before sunrise, in the moment of suspension between darkness and light. The forest and river are shrouded in mist and the sound of the waterfall is muffled. In the half-light Prudence sees many paths leading to her. She is suffering, empty, groping. Is it lust for self-destruction that she feels or desire for re-creation? She lifts a mat of vegetation from the river's edge and her flesh begins to come to life, "pregnant with possibilities".

Suddenly she is back in her room in the house on the hill being cared for by Rakka, her husband's Amerindian servant and mistress, of whom she is of course jealous, although Roi Solman, the husband, is now dead, killed a year after their marriage in a "collision" at the falls. Their baby too has died. Prudence knows that she has suffered a nervous breakdown, but she feels sure that what she has lifted from the river, the "One" (p. 15) in her arms, is not a hallucination. (Neither she nor the reader understands what the "One" is at the time.) Prudence feels there is the possibility of re-creation of herself through a confession of weakness, through humility; what makes it possible for her attitude of self-righteous privilege to give way is that one blow on top of the other has broken her rigidity. She opens her eyes, looks at Rakka, and smiles. Only when the novel is read and reread does the reader see that Prudence in the prelude is the picture of humanity at this moment of civilization's crisis, when it must decide whether it has the will to change its conceptions of life in order to survive.

In the main body of the work, in the search for her own significance and real desires, Prudence searches the paths which have led to her. The principal figure in her past is her father, Henry Tenby, head of a Guyanese middle-class family until his death in 1957. He is the novel's symbol of the dominant outlook and way of life of the first half of the twentieth century.

As a young man travelling in Europe shortly after the First World War, Tenby has fallen in love with Isabella, the golden "muse of the century" who attracts him with her "scent of the chase" (p. 89). She gives an illusion of beauty and of wealth but in truth she is hungry inside, and without any real substance. Like the seemingly rich century, she is covered in glamorous drapery which hides a body of poverty. In England she vanishes, leaving Tenby with ambivalent feelings of love and hate.

He returns to Guyana in the 1920s, the postwar depression years. There upon an earlier "Rakka" he conceives three children, years before their actual birth. They are the mental conceptions of Tenby's life, the principles (or lack of them) by which he lives until the moment of his death.

The first to be thus conceived is Prudence (although she is the last actual child, born in 1940). She is conceived mentally while Tenby is shopping for his "mask of a lifetime" in the "Brothel of Masks", the place where flesh and blood are devalued and imagination is traded for gold. Tenby's conception is of a narrow prudence. He determines that he will, when he marries, live only for his family. Therefore, he, a historian, vows silence, to protect, as he believes, the welfare of his future family. He will avoid, in his historical accounts, explaining the stranglehold he sees that history has had on Rakka. (The name Rakka is used for a woman in each generation, of one race or another, who is used but neglected, and held in the lowest esteem.)

One with whom the Rakkas are equated is Tenby's son Hugh Skelton (skeleton in the closet) who is the dark-skinned member of this "civilized" family in Guyana. Hugh is conceived in Tenby's mind in 1924, year of depression and malaria, of strikes, lockouts, riots, the killing of thirteen strikers by the police, and of concern by the taxpayers about the budget! Hugh is "conceived" in fear, for Tenby is fearful of confrontation with the stark realities of humanity shackled. So out of fear he conceives the ideal of "refinement" and determines that in his account of the times he will hide all things that are socially unacceptable. Out of the coward's attitude that Tenby adopts comes, as a natural result, the hard life of the actual Hugh Skelton; he is always hidden when company comes because his skin is dark; he has the hardest chores in the family; and he is eventually killed in the riots against the budget in 1962, by a bullet inscribed, "This bullet fired by your father's rich kith and kin – all races of endeavour – white + brown + black" (p. 120).

Tenby's third "pre-conception" is his daughter Pamela, the first of these three to be actually born to Tenby and his European-Creole wife Diane, a woman who seems poised and knowledgeable but who is really filled with anxieties and knows nothing. Pamela is conceived – not physically but in abstraction – in 1926, a year of drought, when difficulty and squalor are too much for Tenby to bear. He does not resist measures by the Crown to muffle and disqualify a Popular Party, as later in 1953 he will be apathetic to the suspension by the British of the constitution. His abstraction from the struggles of the day leads to his purely abstract conception of a "model" of purity and innocence, of perfection supposedly. His daughter Pamela later plays her "model" role so well that she marries into the affluent society of the United States. (Richardson's novel, *Pamela or Virtue Rewarded,* probably contributed her name.) But in the United States, in order to remain accepted by this "model" society, Pamela must sacrifice the dark child to whom she too gives birth. Only in this way is she able to escape the US ghetto and live her "model" life. The sacrifice of the grandchild is the result of Tenby's acceptance of the imposed values of his society.

Of Tenby's three children only Prudence is "reconceived" – long after her father's death. The seeds of her rebirth are planted at the moment of his death which results from a heart attack following a collision on the road (between head and heart? reality and appearance?). His imagination, on which he has kept reins all his life, now takes over and he becomes at death a "creature cloven in two, one face on top mask-like as before, the other face beneath emerging from the old" (p. 45). Prudence is alone with him when he staggers into the house. His mask falls – the mask of his age – and she sees the agonized face beneath. It is a traumatic experience for her, but it has beneficial effects years later when she looks back into her past and is able to reconstruct the real meaning of her father's life and time. She is assisted by Tenby's hidden manuscripts he does not have time to destroy.

Prudence comes to understand him as representative of Man in the age of individualism and free enterprise, who is in truth as unfree as possible. Placarded by history as being the soul of freedom, he wears chains of gold upon his heart and wrist. Prudence's feeling for him years later is a feeling of compassion. She sees him as unable to advance far beyond the limits of the past out of which he came. She sees both him and her husband Roi as manifestations of Man in the two major periods of this century, the periods following each of the world wars:

> Each age his expression altered within everything, family as well as nation – cradle as well as grave – crumpled into dust and yet was miraculously restored, rehabilitated by generations of folly, hope. Strange legendary dead and yet unborn spirit he was for each changing day . . . Never the same. Always the same. (pp. 99–100)

History seems a hopeless business if generation after generation is still chained to the primitive past, but it is not entirely hopeless since the evolutionary process which Harris sees at work in history is one in which sudden leaps occur; and who can tell when there will emerge, "out of a spring that was poisoned – ONE who had spent but a night beneath the unequal burden of time" (p. 100), and who will be Man reborn, transformed and united.

At the other extreme of the earlier generation (the underprivileged extreme) is the mother of the Amerindian Rakka. She has refused to join her daughter in the house of Roi Solman, the engineer-technologist. She keeps to the old nomadic way. Her life is a life of squalor and her line also seems without a future, since Rakka is thought to be barren. What Rakka's mother has done, however, is "endure" in both senses of the word: she has endured (suffered) and she has endured (survived). She therefore has something to contribute to the "One" of the future – a core of strength.

Roi Solman (King Sun-man?), the engineer husband of Prudence, seems to represent the post–Second World War period, to 1967. His is the objective, realistic mind. He is intelligent, and learns from experience. In fact, a shock in 1962 (year of the first race conflicts in Guyana) has given him a new insight into the problems of his time. He is capable of recognizing the truth about the poor whom he uses in his work, that they have been made use of "in the name of emancipation, science, industry, all rolled into one – self-interest" (p. 34). But he tells Prudence not to worry: "It's too late to change course now. Poverty is our wealth" (p. 34). It is a collision course that he, like our age, is following, but since he does not know how to avoid it, he has developed a sardonic sense of humour to protect himself. His laughter is his attempt to gain immunity from suffering. His clowning absurdity is his fetish against evil. Partly Amerindian, he feels that the Amerindians represent "the conscience of our age. In this part of the world anyway" (p. 35). He admits that he is tormented at the thought of their plight. Yet "they yield . . . a profit" (p. 35). He tries to maintain a delicate balance, tries to maintain his supremacy. "One cannot tolerate breakdown in day to day rule" (p. 36). So, in the name of self-preservation he rubs his nose on the rock, symbol of the "petrified" (in two senses) establishment.

Roi resembles Tenby in many ways. He too keeps a tight rein on his compassion and imagination. He too acts for Prudence, sacrificing others and himself in her name. He is shown to be like the ancient "divine king" whose life, it was believed, had to be sacrificed when there came a breakdown in the life of the people. But Harris implies that no such outworn primitive rituals and idolatries can save twentieth-century Man, who must himself accept the responsibility for his fate, not shift it to any god or gods. No sacrifices will help except the sacrifice of outworn conceptions, such as the idea that the world is inevitably made up of hunter and hunted. The only hope of survival lies in more deeply scientific knowledge of nature and its processes and in the renewal of man's own creative power. Man himself must be the creator of the new Man. His future depends on himself.

In her recollections of her husband Prudence sees his role in history as that of both hunter and hunted. He is in pursuit of and pursued by contradictions. She sees him doomed in one sense: "Doomed to fall she felt: to collide – to be decapitated like an outworn model. To be sublime, however – a forerunner – an outrider of storm . . . For the pith and core of his sun lay in illumining a structure of relationships" (p. 81). If Mankind is to be reborn, it will be because he could learn so much from this age.

Last in the cast of this Harris "drama of consciousness" is the band of Indians Prudence sees early in the novel. They are a primitive South American tribe whom Prudence has hardly known existed, but with whom she senses identity, as gradually she does with all the characters. The Indians' corial on the river (of time) and her house on the hill are "loci of communi-ty . . . two points high and low – and yet . . . inseparable" (p. 32). The tribe have lost their original vision; she feels that she has too. When she sees them the second time, they cry to her to be born again through her, "expelled from the bandage of history" (p. 49). She – her age – is their last hope. They stop, then plunge to read the summons of life or death. Suddenly, in their life or death is implied the life or death of all, for they too represent not only their own age but mankind and his original sleeping genius, still surviving but in danger of disappearing. The survival of the band of Indians depends on whether she will find and assimilate them and what they mean. They are all that is most alien to this century, it would seem, yet something of the spirit they have lost is what she must find or rediscover beneath the blanket of his-tory. Their original fresh vision must be incorporated into her new vision.

In *Tumatumari*, then, the central figure or symbol is Man himself, in his manifestations in various periods in his whole history, during which he has lived in many different societies and within the wider environment of nature – within the womb of space and time. The title of *Tumatumari* derives from the idea of nature and its processes in time (Tumatumari is said to mean "sleeping rocks"). The scene of Tumatumari suggests that in time even rocks crack, and imaginations awaken, and sudden leaps in development take place.

In contrast, the titles of the five subdivisions of the book derive from social forms and concepts, those that have lasted beyond their time, that once were meaningful, perhaps, but which now are death-dealing. They rep-resent old ideas that can have meaning now not as binding, rock-like tradi-tions and idolatries, but only as "transformed and transforming" tradition, meaningful for this age. For example, Man's major social preconception of life as the game or the hunt needs to be reconceived. The old concepts may once have had the validity of growing out of their appropriate levels of historical development; they were once not ideas imposed by a dead past on early man but concepts original with him (even if mistaken) and growing out of his own experience. It is the originality and independence of spirit that is still valid and not the long outworn interpretations of life and nature. Today Man needs to evaluate, test and change "each given situation" to keep pace, if possible, with life as it changes; he needs to look to the farthest horizon he can perceive from the vantage point of our age. Only such an outlook holds any promise of a future for Man. Rigid adherence to old rock-bound tradition will doom him.

In the novel as a whole ideas of what is rigid and barren are contrasted implicitly with ideas of what is fertile or capable of becoming so. It would be possible to do an interesting study of the images of things barren (like the rich man's penis in a "permanent erection" resulting from fear, that is unable to find release and *give* new life), things fertile (like all the many wombs in the novel) and things capable of changing and becoming fertile (symbolized by the flowering gorgon's head) in order to see the way in which the imagination of Wilson Harris "perceives" ideas and expresses them in art. Some of the reading difficulty is diminished when the reader, like the writer, begins to see these correlations and relationships of imagery.

In spite of the almost indescribable difficulty of *Tumatumari* as a whole, large sections of it read along smoothly enough, and many passages can be enjoyed for their sheer sensuous beauty (while others read like the output of a computer). The novel can be read simply as "experience"; in fact this novel, like all of Harris's novels, should be read for the first time in just this way and not primarily for the intellectual pleasure of it. What will happen with this kind of relaxed approach to it is that some of the underlying philosophical significance will gradually come through to provide illumination for subsequent readings in which intellectual perceptions and sense perceptions will be united.

Many aspects of the novel that seemed to stand out as flaws in early readings of *Tumatumari* took on an essential logic and authority of their own in subsequent readings, although this reader continues to find unsatisfying Harris's way of handling, in a kind of lecture exposition, the "moment of articulation" by the character who has plumbed his own depths and arrived at a new conception of himself and the world (Christo in *The Whole Armour,* the lover in *The Waiting Room,* and to a lesser extent Prudence in *Tumatumari*). In his essays Harris speaks of the need for writers to discover new, fresh potentialities of language. Harris, himself, in all his works, shows that he is capable of making such discoveries. What better occasion is there for him to use this ability than in giving expression to the moment of illumination in the mind of the central character?

Some of the philosophical implications of the novel raise certain questions in the mind of this reader: Is it possible to see the present crisis of mankind rightly, if we view him as one solid mankind only? Doesn't the use of a single figure like Tenby or Roi to represent mankind in successive ages imply that there is but a single human consciousness and experience in each age? Who, in the recent period, would represent mankind in the age of colonialism – the man of the British middle class, for example, or the man of African origin struggling for freedom in Kenya? Is there not a necessary complementary approach to Harris's anthropological one if we are to see the fullest realities of an age, an approach that shows the movement of history in that age as not only part of the overall rhythm of history, but as the result also of the internal dynamic encounters and interactions of *separate* people or groups of people with often conflicting experiences, consciousnesses and feelings? (This is the reality that *The Waiting Room* illustrates.) And do changes of attitude grow within consciousness or memory without constant interaction between it and the world and events outside it? Tenby and Roi are seen in relationship with the events of their age; why is Prudence portrayed as changing in interaction with memory alone?

But even if this point is valid, that an additional view of history is needed to supplement Harris's view in which mankind is assumed to have a representative consciousness and experience before the unity of man, in this sense, is achieved, yet the question is of minor importance in relation to *Tumatumari* with its stimulating wealth of ideas and the contact it makes possible with Harris's rare mind and imagination and his commitment to Man.

There is a statement by the physicist de Broglie that seems almost meant to apply to this work:

> Often the feeling of the imminence of a danger gives birth in the heart of men to sentiments . . . which can serve to avoid it . . . Confronted by the dangers . . . man has need of a "supplement of soul" and he must force himself to acquire it promptly before it is too late. It is the duty of those who have the mission of being the spiritual or intellectual guides of humanity to labour to awaken in it this supplement of soul.[2]

It is as if, in *Tumatumari,* the imagination of Wilson Harris is responding to this call.

Chapter 4

Wilson Harris and
Twentieth-Century Man

"Dear Reader, (THE JUDGE WROTE HALF IN THE MARGIN OF HIS BOOK AND HALF ON A VACANT CARD.) My intention, in part, is to repudiate the vicarious novel . . . where the writer . . . claims to enter the most obscure and difficult terrain of experience without incurring a necessary burden of authenticity, obscurity or difficulty at the same time."[1] So begins a letter from the novelist/judge through whom Wilson Harris speaks in *Ascent to Omai*. It concludes with a reference to the undertaking the writer *does* believe in: "the formidable creative task of digesting and translating our age" (p. 97).

From bits like this in the novels and from Harris's essays and talks, we grasp that he does not want to write simplifications of individual experience from some one-sided point of view. His extraordinary aim is to create in his art an equation in language of the many interacting levels of human consciousness, to draw up from its depths a vision of the possibility of a new conception of man by man in this age of humanity's deepest crisis and disunity. In working towards this aim he has developed a highly symbolic language which has become more and more different from ordinary language as the novels go on. Each word in a Harris novel counts, like an essential brush stroke in a painting, an indispensable note in a complicated musical composition, or an unalterable sign in a mathematical or chemical formula. His art, then, is inevitably difficult, open to many approaches by the reader, saying different things to different people. One reader or critic may look at it through the window of myth, another of mysticism, another of political, philosophical or psychological theory, another of use of language and another of aspects of the imagination. Infinitely many windows on the universe of Wilson Harris must exist. Since that universe resembles in its complexity the universe in which we live, and since it is in constant process of re-creation, no one approach can give a true sense of what the totality contains and implies. But taken all together the interpretations constitute a fellowship of critical imaginations which, as it grows and interacts with Harris's own critical theory, may serve to reveal – to the degree that anything outside the actual fiction can – more of what is involved in his integrated thought and art. My present contribution to this critical fellowship will be to focus on what comes through to me most clearly in the work as a whole – his response to our age: his response to twentieth-century Guyana and to the twentieth-century world and his close relation to some of the ways of thinking and some basic theories of twentieth-century science.

When the English critic F.R. Leavis described the poet as the man most alive in his time, he could not have imagined a Wilson Harris, but – with the modification I think Harris would make of this idea – it seems an apt description of him. The modification would be this: that an age is not a discrete and static thing to be caught and grasped, but is part of a tide arising in the past and always moving towards a future already forming within it. To be alive in one's time, then, would be to have a sense of both the time and the tide.

Guyana was the scene of Harris's contact with our age for thirty-eight years. Everything in his novels, even so abstract a subject as the nature of human consciousness, as in *The Eye of the Scarecrow*, or the relationship of dialectical opposites, as in *The Waiting Room*, or the seeing of invisibilities as in the novel set outside of Guyana, *Black Marsden*, is related, I think, to his response to the human situation in Guyana as he knew it during those years, or as he knew of it in the years since 1959 when he went to live in England.

It is a land of many separations – of race from race, of old from new, of rural areas from town, of coast from interior, of country from continent, of privilege from unprivilege, and often of one aspect of the individual personality from the other. A united independence movement after the Second World War lasted long enough to arouse in many a yearning for unity and the creative things that could come of it. Then, after its electoral victory in 1953, it split. The violent "disturbances" of 1962, 1963 and 1964, mainly between those whose ancestors were brought from Africa and those whose parents and grandparents came as indentured labour from India, made the divisions wider and feelings more set and bitter.

It was in Guyana that the predicament of modern man impressed itself upon Wilson Harris. In spite of the fact that jungles and savannahs may seem to us out of this world, Guyana has in this century and especially since the Second World War been very much a crossroads of the world. It was there that Harris, in seeking a way out of the predicament of twentieth-century man, found in the landscape of the interior both a metaphor for the interior of the person and symbols from nature to represent underlying elements in man's predicament. Rivers, rocks, waterfalls, become symbols: sometimes of frozen conceptions and division and sometimes of illumination, transformation and unity. Harris's first published work, the poems *Eternity to Season* printed privately in Guyana in 1954, is revealingly subtitled "Poems of Separation and Reunion".

The resemblance between the Guyanese predicament and the general predicament of man in the modern world is plain, though the particular factors that go into the dilemma of each are not identical. "Separation" is also the key word in regard to the world today – ever more so, ironically, Wilson Harris says somewhere, as the world supposedly grows smaller. All of Harris's novels imply the world. The early ones do this implicitly in the sense that they deal with man, not with Guyanese man uniquely. The later ones deal explicitly with the world and man in the twentieth century, whether the scene is Guyana, Brazil, Scotland, or some unnamed city of vehicles, pavements and shop windows far from Guyana where most of *The Waiting Room* appears to be located.

Even *Palace of the Peacock,* which is so *visually* a depiction of Guyana's interior, is about man in a world where the various parts of himself are divided from, and forgotten by, each other, in generation after generation. The action is a dream of what could be, the vision coming at the end of a reverse voyage upstream to the source of life, to the original creative, imaginative force in man – a remembering, that is, of what it means to be man. What happens in *Palace of the Peacock* in *death* has meaning only for *life.* The unity which man, represented by the crew, had been forever seeking, the self-fulfilment in the reunion of the various parts of himself, had always been his to take and make part of life; man has eternally possessed this potentiality.

As early as *The Far Journey of Oudin* there are echoes, not only suggested but spoken, of the atomic age. Passages link the events in rural Guyana to the state of the world. Ram says,

> "Don't worry yourself unduly, Mohammed. Everybody story always look bad when they start trotting out misfortune. You passing through a terrible lonely trial of strength and you mustn't feel bad if you don't know how to face the whole story. The world is powder keg, man, Why the newspapers say communists penetrating this country from Russia and everybody is to be called 'comrade'."
>
> "What you mean?"
>
> "I mean you family is not the only one dying out, Mohammed. You is not the only man frighten of being lonely and disinherit in the future. The other day," Ram continued, "look what happen. We talking international story of 'comrades' so let we talk." He saw Mohammed was leaning towards him. "Korea – a country just like this I would say" – he waved his hand generously – "split in half, man. What a mix-up family story. God know who is killing who. You is not the only one in this new family trouble. And what happening to you is *private, plain* AND *ordinary* compared to that."[2]

Whatever Ram's reason for saying these things, the author's reason for having him introduce these matters is to relate the characters and events of the novel to the world.

Tumatumari deals specifically with the contradictions of the twentieth century. Here the "drama of consciousness" takes place within the mind and memory of Prudence, this novel's symbol of the soul of man in the last part of the twentieth century. In a time of personal breakdown she puts together the story and meaning of her father, Henry Tenby, and of her husband, Roi Solman. The former represents the twentieth century between the two world wars, and the latter represents it from the Second World War to his death in 1967, the year the novel was written. In descending into the well of the past, Prudence finds what has gone into her own making. Just after the First World War, her father had fallen in love with the golden "muse of the century", who attracted him with her "scent of the chase".[3] Though she gave an illusion of beauty and wealth, she was really hungry inside, like the seemingly rich century, and in this respect she was like the woman the father eventually marries. Prudence is first conceived by her father, years before her actual birth, as he is shopping for his "mask of a lifetime" in the "Brothel of Masks" where flesh and blood are not valued and imagination is traded for gold. His *conception* of her is of a very narrow prudence. He will sacrifice everything for material security. A historian, he vows silence to protect the welfare of his future family. He hides things in history that are unacceptable in ruling circles as he hides his dark-skinned son when company comes. The son is eventually killed in the riots of 1962. A dark-skinned grandchild is also sacrificed because of Tenby's idolatry of imposed values. And Tenby himself is sacrificed. He dies of a heart attack after a "collision" on the road. His imagination, on which he has kept a rein all his life, takes over right before his death, and Prudence sees him with his mask on top, his real, agonized face emerging beneath it. After his death Prudence finds manuscripts which contain his suppressed thoughts.

Prudence's husband follows a similar course. He is an engineer who exploits the Amerindians even though he sees them as the conscience of the age. Like her father, Prudence's husband keeps a rein on his imagination and compassion. He hides behind sardonic humour. Clowning absurdity is *his* fetish against evil. He too sacrifices himself and others in the name of Prudence. In her recollections of her husband Prudence sees his role in history as that of both hunter and hunted. He is in pursuit of, and pursued by, contradictions. She comes to see him as having been doomed in one sense, "Doomed to fall . . . to collide . . . to be decapitated like an outworn model. To be sublime, however – a forerunner – an outrider of storm . . . For the pith and core of his sun lay in illuminating a structure of relationships" (p.

81). If mankind is to reconceive itself, it will be because it will learn so much from this age, from the contradictions which reveal its needs and unrealized potentialities.

Prudence has lost her child. It is as if there can be no future mankind capable of survival if life is to be no more than an extension of the primitive past, the still-primitive present – primitive in that it sees things in extremes, incapable of sensing that it is possible to bridge the gap by fruitful association, thus bringing forth new forms now "bound in subjection", as Harris says elsewhere.

In the end Prudence's old ideas break down. She sees the possibility of conceiving herself anew, this time as *prudence* in a new fully human sense. *Tumatumari* ends with the thought that mankind can play a new game, "Game of the conception. The great game" (p. 156).

Like Harris's work as a whole, *Ascent to Omai* could be entitled "Of Time and This Time". A drawing by the judge of horizons which widen in his personal memory hints also at significant moments of transition in the history of mankind. Twentieth-century man, looking back to trace the genealogy of his age, finds that "repression, depression, oppression" – and hence catastrophe – have piled up, and now it is raining blood (*Ascent to Omai*, p. 47). Now we are in an age of "global civil war", of non-feeling (*the* crime against humanity), of uncreative "heights of the banal" (p. 85) – an age in which all are slaves to something, and security is a toy of the "manufacturers of unfreedom". The novel contains and also *is* an omen of a crash. Will man heed the sign and his own intuition, remember back to "the womb of mercy from which he had sprung" (p. 29) and be reborn as his own saviour?

In the latest novel, *Black Marsden*, twentieth-century civilization is at the heart of the book. It is on trial for the "nightmare body of wealth" it has accumulated. Nature, earlier times and other cultures have showered it with "gifts, resources, materials beyond the wildest dreams of societies in earlier centuries. Its technological *hubris* has invited a backlash from those cultures which had given all they possessed and from 'nature' which had been drained of so much."[4] It is the age of the consumer, ingesting all, digesting nothing, choking on its wealth. Pressures have built up across generations of disease, starvation, alarming pollution, overpopulation. To one part of man in this age, the other part is invisible though it comes within his range of physical sight, either directly or by means of the camera. It is an age when "millions are eclipsed at starvation point or vanished in Hiroshima" (p. 30). Such things happen in a barren desert of human consciousness; as Marsden says, "Without the desert . . . in which life has become meaningless or extinct, where would we research our A-Bombs?" (p. 31). We have not learned from the "endless oscillations between extremes in the past", and so we follow the same fruitless pattern of uprising followed by repression, repression followed by uprising, the "rat-race of history" (p. 73). Looking at this from the viewpoint of man as man, nothing truly revolutionary has happened for centuries. Nothing really new has been conceived. And the twentieth century is the Dark Ages still (p. 39). At the end of the novel Clive Goodrich refuses to be made into an instrument of this endlessly repetitious past. He is left standing "alone, utterly alone, as upon a post-hypnotic threshold" (p. 111), like every other Wilson Harris representation of modern man. He is ready to move out of the fixed "charmed circles" of imposed thought, "to opt for life as a never-ending river of sweetness, fountain of love" (p. 104). So *Black Marsden,* like the earlier novels, only more explicitly, is about the crisis and trial of the imagination of man in the twentieth century. Like them it develops in fiction the idea of modern man presented openly in the essays, that is – and I am stringing along phrases from the essays now – man in whose psyche there is a great cleavage between the camps and races of himself, who stands "on the brink of a great change or equally great disaster",[5] who must arrive through a drama enacted in his consciousness at a vision of "how weak is the classical architecture of the world and how terrible is the necessity for a new architecture" (*Tradition, the Writer and Society,* p. 8). This vision is the necessary prelude to a new architecture and a new more human being whom man himself must conceive and create. In this respect, all of Harris's novels are preludes, preludes to action, for the implication is that until the new conception of what is needed comes, no truly significant, no truly revolutionary action or change will be possible.

There is a special aspect of our age to which Wilson Harris is most alive, and that is twentieth-century science. His own imagination is one which is both scientific and poetic. The large general aim of twentieth-century science is in large measure his aim. His approach to problems is very much like the approaches of modern science. And specific theories in various sciences seem to have affected him and his art.

Many times over he implies that the solution of the problem of transforming man's consciousness, and hence human existence, requires the contribution of both science and art. "Man will never pass beyond prehistoric conditions until all his gods have failed, and their failure opens up the necessity for self-knowledge and for the scientific understanding of his environment," he writes in the essay "Form and Realism in the West Indian Artist" (p. 17). *Ascent to Omai* speaks of science and art as agencies one of the other. In *Tumatumari* art and science are "overlapping spheres" (*Tumatumari*, p. 30). "Tradition and the West Indian Novel" and *The Eye of the Scarecrow* both make reference to the "poetry of science".[6]

This appreciation of science by an outstandingly creative artist is in itself a significant contribution to the thinking of our day which all too often equates science with the narrowest technology and thinks of it as the arch-enemy of the artistic imagination. Wilson Harris's work shares in what the biologist, Nobel laureate Jacques Monod, describes in *Chance and Necessity* as the ultimate aim of the whole of science, the clarification of "man's relationship to the universe".[7] And Harris's idea of what that relationship is, is essentially the same as that of modern science. The only intelligent purpose in the universe uncovered by science is man's purpose. Though science sees man on the one hand as an accidental product of an indifferent universe, it also sees him as the animal with unique potentialities of rational thought, foresight, poetic imagination and feelings of compassion. He is the only consciously creative force we know. The things we value most, like art and language, are his creation. And only he can form a conception of what he wants to be, and in that sense be his own creation. Wilson Harris says much of this in a few lines in the essay "Form and Realism in the West Indian Artist". After asking who or what is the creator of man, he says, "Man is frequently overwhelmed by the immense and alien power of the universe. But within that immense and alien power the frail heartbeat of man is the never-ending fact of creation" (*Tradition, the Writer and Society*, p. 20).

The creative scientific imagination of our time and the creative imagination of Wilson Harris concern themselves with the same *kinds* of questions. Both study what lies beneath appearances: underlying structures, rhythms and processes, relations between and among phenomena. Both are concerned with such philosophical questions as permanence and change, the discrete and the continuous, the abstract and the concrete, the finite and the infinite, necessity and chance, the interplay of opposites, the basic contradictions and the dynamics of change, and the mysterious harmony and unity scientists in general and Wilson Harris feel exists in the universe. Both imaginations, that which characterizes the creative minds of modern science and that of Wilson Harris, function to a considerable degree in the same way. Both consciously combine symbols in order to make abstract constructions that represent aspects of reality, establishing among things correlations and unsuspected resemblances. Both rely heavily on intuition. Both face the unknown with humility. Each knows there are limitations to the power of reason. Both, however, have faith that the harmony they believe to exist in the universe is increasingly accessible to us and that the understandings we arrive at have philosophical and moral significance, that many of them have the potentiality of bringing about new outlooks and great change.

Wilson Harris shares with theoretical scientists of our age, though not with them alone, the belief that there is always something new in the world, that everything material is constantly moving and changing, that invisible realities beneath appearances cannot be wholly known, partly because of the one-sided bias of the observer but also because things can only be known in their relationships and these are not only endlessly complex and proliferating but *also* ever changing. It is not possible, as *The Waiting Room* puts it, ever to be dead in step with "the swift runner of life".[8] We are especially deceived when we try to isolate something in order to examine it. Then, Harris says, we arrest a "web of processes" (p. 67). For, as modern science knows, the properties of things exist only in relationship. In *The Waiting Room,* this concept, that only in relationship can things be known, and especially in the association of opposites, is conveyed by the sex imagery throughout.

Relativity physics finds that different observers have different time scales which depend on their motion. The time scale is intimately related to space in a time–space continuum. Time and space do not have separate existences apart from matter but rather are aspects of matter. Wilson Harris's related concepts began to appear early – always, of course, interwoven with his other meanings. In one of the poems in *Eternity to Season*, entitled "The Glorious Children of the Gods", we read:

> For time is no fixed boat or inevitable doom
> but is the motion of men and matter in space, subtly
> flowing and binding into universal action, into construction,
> into related texture and interaction, into function and
> > formation,
> mortality and immortality, all one substance
> moving and making time.[9]

In quantum physics the idea of complementarity is of great significance. The phenomenon of light must be viewed alternately in two contradictory ways, as corpuscles *and* as waves. Each view alone is incomplete, the full reality being revealed only in the association of the two views. Analogous to this idea is Harris's concept that we find reality only in the association of antagonistic principles. It is first introduced in the essay "Art and Criticism" (1951), in the passage reacting to that school of West Indian art which idealizes the sun: "I have lived for long periods in savannahs so much exposed to heat and fire, that the sun has become an adversary – one of two antagonistic principles – night and day – and only an association of these principles provides release" (*Tradition, the Writer and Society*, p. 10). In this instance the antagonistic principles are night and day, but readers of Wilson Harris will be reminded of all the other pairs that appear in the novels, usually joined by a slash: fire/ice, subjective/objective, material/immaterial, positive/negative, up/down, left/right and so on, all so-called opposites necessary to each other in a dynamic interrelationship which alone can generate new creation.

Wilson Harris's idea that immaterial form is primary and material content secondary may appear at first to be simply Platonic idealism or a yearning for another world of spirit only. It will then appear to be in contradiction to his clear affirmation of the concrete in *The Waiting Room* and elsewhere; to the idea that value should be conceived in terms of "flesh and blood, not spirit and stone", and to the repudiation of a "total paradise" in *The Age of the Rainmakers*. But on closer examination, his idea of the primacy of form is found to parallel the modern scientific interpretation of form in living beings as explained in a passage from *Science in History* by the physicist and historian of science, J.D. Bernal: "What is permanent, then, in an individual life is not the matter but the forms and reactions of the molecules out of which organized beings are made. The actual matter seems to be essential mainly because it is needed to execute the continual cycles of chemical changes which are life."[10] So, while matter is *needed* and form cannot exist apart from it, the form, the process, is the permanent thing and the particular matter only temporary. Heisenberg, the nuclear physicist, makes the point about the primacy of form in this way: "The elementary particle, like the stationary state of an atom, is determined by its symmetry . . . I am quite fascinated by the idea that symmetry should be something much more fundamental than the particle itself."[11] Heisenberg's illustration is a splendid one to illustrate also Wilson Harris's idea that form is basic.

Closely connected with the idea of the *material* and the idea of the *immaterial* is the idea of matter as congealed energy. Is it too wild an idea that the animal which is related to the light of the sun at the end of *Palace of the Peacock* is energy made visible: "The animal was so lithe and swift . . . It bounded and glanced everywhere, on the table, on the windowsill with the dying light of the sun, drawing itself together into a musing ball. It danced around the room swift as a running light, impetuous as a dream. It was everywhere and nowhere, a picture of abandonment and air, a cat on crazy balls of feet. It was the universe . . ."[12]

As a last example of Wilson Harris's way of appropriating for his own uses ideas from modern science, there is this beautiful passage from *Tumatumari* which ends with specific reference to knowledge derived from historical geology:

> The sun was high in the sky when Roi began to ascend the hill with the boar he had slain on his back. The clouds had vanished and the line of the mountains appeared now like a lofty crest of water breaking its own wave ceaselessly – undulating and refracting. It was a curious impression – the vast waving outline of the mountains

and the transparent ocean of the sky within and beneath which fell away other exposures, shorelines, crests and seas like interior jungles of oceanic worlds, vegetation as well as sand – tier after tier, rank after rank of bush, descending balconies as in a submerged amphitheatre upon one of the lowest rungs of which Roi climbed . . . The heatwaves upon sand and forest were intense: they remoulded and shattered everything – rising and falling contours – fluid/solid – water/fire – cauldron of space . . . *In truth the ocean had once crawled here upon an ancient continental shelf and climbed still higher beyond Tumatumari to its farthest limit – the escarpment of Kaieteur.* (*Tumatumari*, pp. 53–54)

As the novels go on, the symbols become stranger, the inventions less recognizably like anything we have known before, the juxtaposition and interpenetration of images more startling, and the use of language more and more unusual; but the basic form remains, the dynamical process of human consciousness that Wilson Harris envisions for man as he – man – responds to the need to create a new conception of himself. The strange symbols resemble those of a mathematician who finds that no old symbols convey his new meaning and that he must invent his own. The mathematician defines his use of the symbols; Wilson Harris conveys the meaning of his only by their use in many changing contexts. Thus he forces the reader to do what he espouses – to maintain an openness of mind about reality and to keep his thinking fluid. His images do not have fixed significance. In new contexts, they have new meanings, and their potentialities for further transformation are implied.

The effect on Wilson Harris's art of the idea that everything in the universe is moving and interacting as part of a dynamic system could be demonstrated perhaps endlessly. If one opens a Harris novel to almost any part, one finds all in movement and interaction. The development of *Palace of the Peacock,* for example, could never be conveyed by a series of still pictures or paintings, no matter how beautiful. The *movement* is all. Each moment of a Wilson Harris novel is part of a process of change – of crumbling or reconstitution – leading to a sudden leap in consciousness. Even when a symbol appears to represent the inert, the forever barren, it holds within it the capacity to be transformed, as with the gorgon's head in *Tumatumari* which at the end smiles, "wreathed by the elements" (p. 155), or as with the "gaol" of environment in *Age of the Rainmakers*[13] which eventually becomes a fertile prisonhouse (p. 95).

What finally is likely to be his effect upon the age? In what he calls "the dialogue of culture and civilization", his undertaking is to act as a guide in the building of a community of imaginations dedicated to sensing the needs of humanity and exploring the possibilities of imagination to bring about truly fundamental changes in man's consciousness. Wilson Harris enlarges perspectives, showing the necessity to find alternatives to conventional institutions, attitudes and art. He sets an example of the boldest experimentation and exploration through poetry. Above all, we are caught up in his concern; we are led to wonder whether it is not, after all, possible to achieve the unity of mankind. Wilson Harris, well-known in other parts of the world, is too little known in this country. Yet readers in the United States dearly need to discover him, for his art has the power, like Carroll's music in *Palace of the Peacock*, to touch "the listening harp in every member of the crew" (p. 78).

Chapter 5

Melville and Harris
Poetic Imaginations Related in Their Response to the Modern World

The juxtaposition of Herman Melville and Wilson Harris seems fated; ultimately an exploration of the correspondences and differences in their art had to begin, for between the two a profound kinship exists. I am not alone in sensing this. In his study of *Tumatumari,* Ivan van Sertima, Guyanese poet and critic, says that "no configuration in modern literature, outside of the crew of the Pequod in Melville's *Moby-Dick,* can rival the organic cosmopolis of races, bloods and cultural complexes invoked in the crew of Donne in Harris's first novel *Palace of the Peacock*".[1] The distinguished student of West Indian social, cultural and intellectual history, C.L.R. James, who is also the author of a book (*Mariners, Renegades and Castaways*) on the significance of *Moby-Dick* for modern civilization, values both Melville and Harris for closely related reasons involving insight into the interrelationship of our age, its past and future. And Harris as literary critic and theoretician is deeply interested in Melville, whom he lists first among his examples of native/universal artists. He sees Melville as having been engaged in the re-creation of the epic, which in his mind deals with the "soul" of man. The author's note to the combined edition of *The Whole Armour* and *The Secret Ladder* begins with a reference to Melville's art in *Benito Cereno,* in which short novel, Harris says elsewhere, its author "intuitively caught a tide of events that would loom into the twentieth century".[2] And speaking of the need for a new kind of "heterogeneous" novel to focus on man rather than on supposedly sovereign individual men and women, he finds: "One would have to turn to Melville to sense the beginnings of this kind of thing in the novel."[3]

There is even an omen to betoken the bond between the American/universal novelist and the Guyanese/universal one. If we invert the initials of Herman Melville (HM) or of Wilson Harris (WH) what do we see? The initials of the other! Clearly the juxtaposition *is* ordained. This omen augurs well for a full-scale, continuing exploration of Melville and Harris by a community of critical imaginations. The light from one should throw light on the other; the light from both will, I think, show them together in a new kind of literary and historical perspective.

A few facts, mainly biographical, form the background of my reconnaissance report. Melville was born in 1819 in New York City, once called New Amsterdam; Harris was born in 1921 in another New Amsterdam, this one on the coast of Guyana, then a colony of Britain, a country inhabited by people of many racial, national and religious origins, several of which were often incorporated in the same person, as in the case of Wilson Harris. The striking parallel in personal experience is that both lived for a number of imagination-forming years outside modern civilization and in contact with nature as it had been for millennia – Melville as a sailor on whalers and a man-of-war and living for a short time with native peoples in the South Pacific, and Harris as a surveyor in the interior of Guyana, a territory of jungles, waterfalls, rivers and savannahs. Both, then, had the possibility of seeing the dominant civilization in a fresh perspective. They lived and worked in small, close groups of people of many origins and ways of interpreting life. Both came in contact with so-called primitive people and learned from them. But neither is a primitivist: the native peoples in the South Pacific became for Melville a point of reference from which to see the savagery of the nineteenth-century imperialist world, and the Amerindians who remained outside organized Guyanese society became for Harris a symbol of all those who have been ignored in life, wiped out in recorded history and dimmed in our imaginations – symbol of the obscure person through whose eye we should strive to see, symbol of a past with which we must enter into a new relationship for a necessary renewal of forgotten sympathies and a new conception of man and community. Each poet's experience – at sea or in the Guyana interior – provided symbols which were to be essential elements of his unique vision of the world.

After this earlier period, each turned to writing with all his creative energy. Melville, in a period of over forty-five years, wrote ten novels, one novella, a good number of short stories and much poetry, including the five-hundred-page-long *Clarel.* Wilson Harris has published ten novels with two others on the way, two books of short fiction, the poems in *Eternity to Season,* and essays clarifying his revolutionary literary theory and methods, his interrelated social and literary values and aims.

If Melville's narratives of the South Pacific, *Typee* and *Omoo,* are viewed as two parts of one work, each of his novels is unique in central artistic conception, form and spirit, but his work as a whole expresses a unified philosophy and social outlook. This is true of Harris, too. But more than that, the Harris novels interpenetrate each other; though no story line connects them, they are one ever-evolving work of fiction; ideas spiral outward, and inventions of phrase and image spring up again and again. The art of both novelists has often been taken to be too difficult, their language, associations and symbols too private. Convinced of the depth and complexity of life and the universe, they have worked to convey some of that complexity rather than try to reduce it to simple, less authentic, terms. Nevertheless, when we read their work through its imagery above all, more of its complex meaning comes through with each reading, especially if we refrain from imposing our own conventional ideas of what certain symbols mean; *darkness,* for example, so often presumed to have a pejorative implication, is time after time conceived as the source or symbol of light by both Melville and Harris.

Because each has the kind of imagination which continually reaches out into the universe and the unknown – and in Harris's case far down into the depths of "primordial" memory – and because he regularly occupies himself with philosophical questions, each writer has frequently been misinterpret-

EDINBURGH UNIVERSITY LIBRARY
CANCELLED

ed in that his main concern is often thought to be an "eternal essence", separate and apart from the world of men and from the concrete problems of an age. Many readers, for instance, have the illusion that *Palace of the Peacock* and *Billy Budd* arrive at transcendent visions of eternal, changeless radiance. But both Melville and Harris everywhere say, either directly or indirectly, that nothing is ever complete or perfect or of the spirit alone. For both authors the "visible world of experience", to use Melville's words, is the "pro-creative thing that impregnates the muses".[4] Neither aspires to transcend life; what he seeks is *relation:* between abstract and concrete, death and life, permanence and change, "eternity and season". What *The Waiting Room* calls "the indestructible evanescence of life" interests Harris in his ever-disintegrating and reintegrating universe; the endless, continuous fabric of life in his universe is what Melville pictures in *Moby-Dick.* And at the very centre of each of these universes is man. Ishmael alone on the ocean, surrounded by unbroken sea and sky gives pictorial expression to Melville's feeling about man's centrality. And Harris says of the universe that "within that immense and alien power, the frail heart-beat of man is the never-ending fact of creation."[5] The "complexity of value," he says, "is flesh and blood, not spirit and stone".[6] The motive force in the far-reaching imagination of both Melville and Harris is the desire to find what can illuminate the contemporary world and its need for harmony among men.

Moby-Dick is the most powerful and memorable single expression of that desire for unity in literature, the great symbolic poem of the spirit of war and of peace. Rigid, split, exploiting and self-crucifying Ahab, incapable of seeing himself as only part of man, strips himself of all his humanities and stakes the lives of all in his private war against life, as incarnated in the white whale, in which he can see nothing but evil. He is one potentiality in man, the destructive and self-destructive one. In artistic opposition to him is Queequeg, who embodies all colours of man, all times, all that has ever been valid and has survived uncorrupted by modern civilization, the creative potentiality buried but latent in each of the "mariners, renegades and castaways" of the crew. He stands in creative relation to man, to nature, to his god whom he is forever whittling, and to the unbroken universe into which he will sail after death. He is a breathing image of the spirit Wilson Harris, too, values most in man, and if we did not already know this fantastic creation, a multi-coloured figure with hieroglyphics and nature markings on his body, we would not be surprised to find him in a Harris novel. Ahab takes the crew of the Pequod to annihilation in a scene prophetic of the almost utter destruction possible in our age: "And now concentric circles seized the lone boat itself, and all its crew, and each floating oar, and every lance-pole, and spinning, animate and inanimate, all round and round in one vortex, carried the smallest chip of the Pequod out of sight."[7] But Ishmael, who has been pulled by both Ahab and Queequeg, by both potentialities within him, has been saved by Queequeg's coffin-canoe which shoots up from the centre of the vortex in the sea. He is man's representative reborn to have another chance to conceive a better design of life. At this moment Melville, like Harris at all times, sees with intense poetic conviction that the world may be transformed. His symbols of war are metamorphosed into symbols of peace. Ishmael is held afloat by Queequeg's coffin-canoe – an image related to the Harris funeral/cradle conception – and the world, at least for the symbolic moment, is stunningly transformed: "The unharming sharks they glided by as if with padlocks on their mouths; the savage sea-hawks sailed with sheathed beaks."[8]

Not many scenes in literature can stand beside the ending of *Moby-Dick* as visualization of the idea of transformation to a world at peace, but the climax of *Palace of the Peacock* can. The crew of Donne – the crew *in* Donne, but also another generation in the so far "repetitive boat" of history – has discovered at the moment of death that only in harmony among them can there be fulfilment of their deepest needs. Donne has been a kind of Ahab, a ruler-destroyer driven by pride, who would take all to destruction in his ambition to rule. But to Harris he is, unlike Ahab to Melville, capable of change. For in Harris the "soul", the creative imagination and desire, can be awakened to act in all. In the final movement of *Palace of the Peacock* there unfolds, to reveal the possible metamorphosis of life, a whole sequence of sparkling transformations, each new image pulsating out of the one before:

I saw the tree in the distance wave its arms and walk when I looked at it through the spiritual eye of the soul. First it shed its leaves sudden and swift as if the gust of wind that blew had ripped it almost bare. The bark and wood turned to lightning flesh and the sun which had been suspended from its head rippled and broke into stars that stood where the shattered leaves had been in the living wake of the storm. The enormous starry dress it now wore spread itself all around into a full majestic gown from which emerged the intimate column of a musing neck, face and hands, and twinkling feet. The stars became peacocks' eyes, and the great tree of flesh and blood swirled into another stream that sparkled with divine feathers where the neck and the hands and feet had been nailed.

This was the palace of the universe and the windows of the soul looked out and in. The living eyes of the crested head were free to observe the twinkling stars and eyes and windows on the rest of the body and wings. Every cruel mark and stripe had vanished.[9]

A progression of aural transformations follows, beginning with Carroll's whistling and ending with music that circumnavigates the globe and yet comes from a source far within everyone. The music of the novel ends with the introduction of a theme leading back to life: "Each of us now held at last in his arms what he had been forever seeking and what he had eternally possessed."[10] The spirit at the end of *Palace of the Peacock* and the spirit at the end of *Moby-Dick,* as indeed the spirit of both novels in almost every particular, are in harmony: man has within him the great potentiality for a creative life; he continues to be reborn with yet another chance to realize it; it is conceivable that one day he will transform the design of his life.

Not all of Melville's novels express the belief that change in the pattern of modern civilization will come in the imaginable future. That bitter novel, *The Confidence-Man,* voices near-despair, salvaging only the merest grain of hope, and no Melville novel besides *Moby-Dick* imagines such spectacular change. In contrast, each and every novel by Harris breathes his belief that we live in what could be a gateway age. We could move through it – through an understanding of it – to an era never before conceived of by man. This difference in their outlook reflects a basic difference between the nineteenth and the twentieth century.

It must have seemed to Melville in his period of rising imperialism, industrialization and the growing worship of money that the power of wealth and authority, of institutions and precedents, was – to use a recurrent Harris word – implacable. His art rejects contemporary civilization almost in its entirety, presenting with immense power the realities of war, imperialism, slavery, the extermination by the white man of the American Indian, and the corruption of values in America and everywhere else in modern civilization. Each individual work is a challenge to the reader to seek a way out of the maze. But he himself points no direction.

The twentieth century has seen the horrors accumulate almost to the breaking point of civilization. But it has also witnessed changes – political, economic, social, artistic and intellectual – at a rate so unprecedented that it is now apparent that change *is* the nature of our world. Previously unimagined perspectives have opened up. Science has introduced new ways of looking at phenomena that would once have outraged one's idea of reality. But, above all, the century has presented the ultimatum that civilization *must* change or be destroyed. Harris's art reflects both faces of our age, both its horrors and its possibility of change. He accepts as the present-day novelist's responsibility "the formidable and creative task of digesting and translating our age". Instead of rejecting contemporary civilization, as Melville does, he seeks to look through it to see how its contradictions can be made fertile, how our time can be transformed from a prison into a womb of creative change. What he sees is that the continuation of conceptions of polarized extremes can lead nowhere but to catastrophe, that only in the bringing together of so-called contraries can a new age be conceived. Only then will the schizophrenic gap within man, and within each individual, be bridged. But this can happen only through the sacrifice of "embedded and cherished" habits of thought and feeling perpetuated by frozen tradition, what to Melville are the "marble" forms and precedents.

The imposition by the past of patterns and obsessions which have enslaved, imprisoned, split and victimized everyone is a major theme in all of Melville and Harris. But Harris's main attention is focussed on how the consolidation of the past can be broken down. Like that "half-frozen spectre"[11] which is Black Marsden when Goodrich first comes upon him, the past, a sorcerer with two faces, can be unfrozen to work within the imagination but only if one relates to it in a new way, refusing to be its pawn or to sleepwalk under its hypnotic influence. If Goodrich, who represents twentieth-century civilization in *Black Marsden,* does not resist being fitted into preconceived patterns, he will be led to destruction, something he finally realizes and decides against.

Harris's faith is limitless that a great change in human consciousness *can* take place, that even the shape of things in the domain of the Jungian "archetype of the collective unconscious" can be altered or broken. In fact Christo's flight in *The Whole Armour* seems an "archetypal dream" of desperate flight and fear whose shape *is* broken when Christo stops running and returns to face those he was running from.

There is another aspect of the past in Harris's view, the past which has been buried but which man could bring back to life in his imagination. Always present in Harris's art, the idea is suggested most memorably by Poseidon in *The Secret Ladder,* the ancient leader of the Canje River descendants of freed and runaway slaves who live outside the main stream of Guyanese life. Poseidon is the dynamic which enters into Fenwick's life, awakens his conscience and helps him to begin to conceive human value in a new way.

Harris's view of the two aspects of the past, one sterile and self-perpetuating, the other buried but still potent, leads him to the belief that man needs a new philosophy of history and along with this a new philosophy of revolution to break the pattern of the "rat-race of history", repression followed by uprising, uprising followed by repression, and to bring to a halt the endless rounds of static protest, blind action and self-isolation by those who feel they are the sole victims of the world and who unconsciously cling to that role. On this question the art of both Harris and Melville sets forth these ideas: that *all* are victims of the patterns set by the past; that all have needs not met by the world as it is, and do, even without knowing it, desire to change it; that each consents to his own destruction by letting himself be pushed into an extreme role. Harris alone, however, believes that rigid attitudes can be pierced and new light from the other side enter. It is not my impression that Harris believes that this could have been possible at the time of the slave uprising in *Benito Cereno,* for example, or even in Melville's time, but he does believe that it is possible in our age of crisis for all mankind. He does believe that revolution *can* come *out of a whole people,* and that this is the only really revolutionary possibility. Revolution in his sense implies the achievement of the kind of relationship which will lead to the unity of man. Related to this is his belief that only in man as a whole can any person find his true, fulfilling identity. Also related is his belief in a "marriage of cultures" – Melville's "marriage" of Ishmael and Queequeg.

Harris's dramas are not dramas of individual consciousness alone but also of social consciousness. As he explains, the imagination of Donne in *Palace of the Peacock,* Fenwick in *The Secret Ladder,* and Stevenson in *Heartland* are all agents of one imagination, by which I understand him to mean man's imagination, like the original, still-latent, creative spirit of man Melville envisioned in Queequeg. Drawing on it, and developing it, each individual can share in the revolutionary transformation of society, and the artist and historian can make more creative the interchange between culture and civilization. Harris, in a more critical and rapidly changing time than Melville's, sees the possibility of a qualitative leap in social development, which had not yet ripened in the earlier time. But there is no difference between these writers about what major, specific aspects of the modern world need to be changed, except that Harris confronts and probes conditions which did not exist, or did not exist to the same extent, in nineteenth-century civilization: intense racial conflicts, widespread realization by women of their limiting lives, mass starvation and the actuality of atomic war.

There is much in common in the ways in which Melville and Harris realize ideas and feelings in their art. Both create new visions of the world through which others can then see. Both have a sense of primordial things. Each uses mythic, Christian and literary material of the past for his own original meanings. They are alike in the daring of their art and in its vast range and variety. How often is a Melville or Harris reader spellbound at the beauty of a passage – like the exquisite crystallization of meaning at the end of *Billy Budd* or *The Age of the Rainmakers* – or amazed at the audacity of some grotesque conception – like the Indian-killer *par excellence* in *The Confidence-Man* or Jack History's unrelieved erection in *Tumatumari!* Both use language as the art of exploring values. They create what Harris calls "potent, explosive images" to explode old preconceptions; they bring about bizarre juxtapositions to open up a new vision of things, Harris doing this as a fundamental part of his merged philosophy and art. Both believe in what

Harris terms "the authenticity of narrative as the active medium of ideas". None of their novels lends itself to final interpretation any more than the complex life they probe. As Marsden says, "Lots of intriguing complications here, so be on your guard."[12] Neither ever seems to feel he has ultimate answers. Melville continued to the end of his life to probe the subsurface realities of his world; Harris continues to seek deeper understanding of the relations between consciousness and history, thought and act, *Tumatumari* being an outstanding example of this.

Many of the *differences* in the art of Melville and Harris seem related to the differences in their feelings about change. Each Melville novel takes its shape from its content and unique conception; with Harris it is the other way around – form is primary and the content of each novel develops in accordance with the process of dynamic change which gives the novel its form. Melville's characters, with few exceptions, unchangingly *stand* for what they signify; they have unflickering essences. He sees his opposites as irreconcilable, with disastrous results for all, as in *Benito Cereno*. Harris's men and women are not "polarized identities". No one ever stands for an unchanging quality in Harris's imagination. In his hands even rigid Ahab would be transformable. Melville's art presents vivid, indelible *pictures* symbolizing aspects of the world. In Harris's novels *movement* is memorable: each unforgettable scene is a dissolving part of a "web of processes", in which all is crumbling and reintegrating in each impossible-to-isolate moment. Most of Melville's symbols and images have permanent implications; a single Harris image, like a symphonic theme, is likely to go through an evolutionary process; its implications change from context to context in a continual variation and development until in the end it may be entirely different from what it started out to be. In *Tumatumari* an eye eventually appears and opens in the face of the rock; the gorgon of history begins to smile. Then we see that all along the original image, like the early musical theme, had these possibilities of transformation within it.

Herman Melville and Wilson Harris give us an idea of how the imagination of man can stretch within the possibilities of a time. They are part of a great world literary tradition concerned with all of man in the whole known world. Like Donne, Fenwick and Stevenson, they are both agents of one creative imagination which runs through man and which may help him decide to renounce the destruction and self-destruction which Melville's art as a whole makes so visible and to opt for what Wilson Harris holds out as a dazzling and almost tangible possibility, a new Creation of the world and man by man himself.

Postscript (February 1975)

Since the University of Liege conference a more profound exploration of *Billy Budd,* which I have just completed for the last chapter of my book on Melville and war, has led me to modify in the following respect my view of the similarities and differences between Melville and Harris: In his last work Melville came much closer than I had previously realized to Harris's philosophical and poetic vision of how humanity's original, latent, creative imagination may be awakened to the need for a transformation of the "classical architecture of the world".[13]

Chapter 6

Wilson Harris's *The Womb of Space: The Cross-Cultural Imagination*

The relationship Wilson Harris perceives between the inner world of consciousness/imagination and the world of flesh-and-blood people acting in time and space has always been more directly communicated in his critical essays than in his fiction, though the essays no less than the fiction are expressions of his poetic imagination. They are filled with passion against divisions in humankind and for a vision of an evolved humanity integrated and creative as a result of the fertilization of imagination by the artist, whose responsibility is therefore sacred. Harris's critical theory (a complete break with the usual view of separate regional, ethnic, or national literatures), very much developed and unified in *The Womb of Space*, is his clear expression of this passion for a transformation of the inner *and* outer world. Never before has his perception of universal images central to myths of many places and to many modern novels and poems, created in many parts of the world and in many cultures, been so richly demonstrated. To Harris recurring images of terror, of falling, of pregnancy, of creation, of resurrection, of flying, of metamorphoses, of doubles and twins, of merged animal and human, of harlequin figures, of the "sent dead" as in Haitian *Vodun,* of rainbow bridge and tree linking sky and earth, and other variable images of life-in-death, death-in-life all attest to the ways in which the past can speak to the present and future as well as to people of all cultures. They are images which, because of the "dynamism of metaphor" (Rimbaud), are capable, Harris feels, of changing our ways of relating to others since they reveal "the necessity for community to evolve through complex visions of apparent catastrophe" and the necessity, especially in a time of nuclear war possibility, for a vision of the rebirth of humankind in contrast to the "death of Man" popularized by the French philosopher Michel Foucault and evidenced by widespread nihilist literature, theatre, film and television.

John W. Blassingame and Henry Louis Gates, Jr, give this succinct summary of *The Womb of Space* in their foreword:

> Harris is concerned to show the fundamental unity of the human community, both by underscoring repeated patterns of symbol-making or "figuration" in the world's cultures and art and by revealing the movement from unawareness to consciousness as depicted in the mythic symbol. By discussing texts from the American, Latin American and European literary traditions, Harris analyzes that quality which "mythical" novels share.[1]

It should be added that Harris looks deeply into almost a score of well-known modern works – poetry as well as prose fiction – from the Caribbean, Africa, Australia and Asia, as well as the areas named in the foreword.

In his introduction, Harris compresses the literary philosophy that constitutes a breakthrough in modern critical theory, the latter being so generally negative about the possibility of language to communicate and about the possibility of any shared interpretation. He states the purpose of his "cross-cultural exploration" as an attempt "to bring into play certain disregarded and yet exciting pathways that bear upon cross-cultural capacities for genuine change in communities beset by complex dangers and whose antecedents are diverse".[2] He explains his selection of novels and poems in his exploration (Faulkner's *Intruder in the Dust;* Edgar Allan Poe's *Arthur Gordon Pym;* Ralph Ellison's *Invisible Man;* Jean Toomer's "Box Seat" in *Cane;* Juan Rulfo's *Pedro Paramo;* Jay Wright's *The Double Invention of Komo;*

Jean Rhys's *Wide Sargasso Sea;* Paule Marshall's *The Chosen Place, the Timeless People;* Patrick White's *Voss;* Raja Rao's *The Serpent and the Rope;* Mervyn Peake's *Gormenghast;* Emma Tennant's *The Last of the Country House Murders;* Claude Simon's *The Flanders Road;* Djuna Barnes's *Nightwood;* and several works by poets of the Caribbean, Africa and Asia); he states that he sees them as gateways into the largely submerged territory of the imagination, but that other works could have been chosen: "In this particular study, and within the stresses of exploration rarely undertaken by readers or critics, I had no alternative but to limit my selection in order to highlight variables of dialogue that tend to be suppressed in so-called normal classifications of fiction and poetry within regional scholarship" (pp. xix–xx). The works Harris analyses are related by him not only to the myths, folklore and visual art of earlier times but are continually related, chapter by chapter, to each other through cross-cultural images, thus forming a cross-cultural web that reflects his conception of a "cross-cultural loom". Harris explains that his exploration will start with his reflections on *Intruder in the Dust* since this analysis will clarify at once some of the issues and possibilities involved in a cross-cultural perspective:

> It is unlikely, as we shall see, that Faulkner was aware of how strangely his imagination had been pulled in this novel . . . . Let me dwell a little on the phenomenon of otherness that moves in the novel yet remains curiously beyond Faulkner's vision, so to speak. Had he seen it – had the life of heterogeneity, in unconscious or intuitive dialogue with his creativity come home to him – he would have been driven, I think, to revise the one-sided moral conclusions built into the closing premises of the novel. What perhaps I should say now is that the phenomenon of otherness borders on *the validity of mental images as distinct from intellectual conclusions.* (My italics – J.S.A.) (*Womb of Space*, pp. xvii–xviii)

In the opening chapter to *Tradition, the Writer and Society,* "Reflections on *Intruder in the Dust*", Harris finds that the "barren philosophical climax 'of the work' . . . gives some weight to the charges"[3] often directed against it, but that *Intruder in the Dust* has a capacity "that breaches conventional logic and gives the novel its complicated power and focus" (*Womb of Space*, p. 4). He is struck first by young Mallison's precipitous fall which is an ascent in that it turns the world of the segregated South in the novel upside down; then by the coincidence of Faulkner's fictional events with the Haitian belief in the "sent dead" invoked to destroy the living – a fate countered only by a *hungan* figure who can succeed in making the dead let go; then by the "twins" Faulkner sees (Mrs Beauchamp and Miss Habersham) who have dwelt in separate life-destroying ghettoes, one black and one white, and in the parody of that twinship in the double-headed coffin and elsewhere. To Harris, Faulkner's ending of his novel with a defence of "territorial-in-moral imperative" is an instructive failure, showing how the unconscious creative power of the novelist in this book "freezes and aborts itself" (p. 12). To Harris, "This brings home the reality of evil, in which cultures are enmeshed in codes to invert or overturn each other rather than become involved in complex mutuality and the difficult creation of community" (p. 13). Because this mutuality and community constitute Harris's idea of the goal of imaginative literature, the epic is what he feels the novel should aspire to.

The chapter that follows, "The Schizophrenic Sea", looks back to an earlier work Harris feels to be a forerunner of many self-divided twentieth-century works, *Intruder in the Dust* among them, and that is Poe's *Arthur Gordon Pym.* Again he concentrates primarily not on the author's conscious intention but on his intuitive self as revealed in his images. It is not possible here to outline Harris's analysis of the "schizophrenic genius of Edgar Allan Poe in this strange narrative" (p. 15), except to say that it too features odd twinships between black and white of which Poe must have been unaware and Pym's "Freudian slip" (p. 24) when he refers to himself and Peters as the only *white* men on the island in spite of the fact that he had earlier associated the Amerindian Peters with the "Negro" towards whom Poe had obsessive feelings of aversion (as evidenced by his portraiture of all the black characters in the work) to such an extent that the very teeth of the later "metaphysical blacks" (p. 23), as Harris describes their role, are black, to show them utterly frightening. Harris relates *Pym* to pre-Columbian myths of cannibalism and to distorting reports by Spanish explorers about "cannibal" Indians: "The excesses of Poe's *Pym* begin to yield to judgments and criteria born of the twinship of intuitive self and myth" (p. 26). As I understand it, Harris feels that there is something intrinsic yet still buried in the human species, only as yet momentarily resurrected and seen, and that in *Intruder* and *Pym* these impulses and their related images (such as the twinships of black and white) break through, creating fissures in the authors' partial views "masquerading as totalities" (p. 26).

In Ralph Ellison's *Invisible Man* Harris sees a novel that *is* "epic" in thrust (p. 31). To him it tells of "foetal man" (p. 30) in the womb of an age who neither aborts nor comes to birth, repetitively dying yet psychically reawakening in each phase of the novel, each phase representing one of the "concentric horizons" (p. 28) that give this chapter its title. In *Invisible Man* Harris convincingly sees a blend of Homeric, Anancy (African) and Christian imageries that is "substantial to the womb of evolutionary space that Ellison seeks in dying (awakening) epic god on each horizon or concentric ring" (p. 29). To him the invisible man of the novel is a black Odysseus "in whose fictive musical blood Anancy runs" (p. 30) and who is pursued, as much within his own skull as from without, by Cyclopean "nightmare" (p. 31). Harris makes an outstanding contribution to an understanding of the role of the female characters in the work for he stresses the bleakness of awakenings black Odysseus experiences when the female is consistently disadvantaged (p. 28). Nor does Harris limit this point to black Odysseus for he stresses, too, the need to understand the significance of women in relation to the rainbow arcs or bridges between cultures and by implication between male and female human beings.

The question of the place of women in the minds of men becomes an important element in the chapter "The Untamable Cosmos", playing a major part in the discussion of Rulfo's *Pedro Paramo* and pre-Columbian Mexican myth in which Harris finds Rulfo's fatalism rooted:

> The hidden status of the female in pre-Columbian myth – as well as the conscripted and debased faculty of women in modern fiction – does place, as we have seen in Ellison's major novel, in Toomer and in Rulfo, a bleak capacity upon gestating hero or man/god. So it is not surprising to find that ideologies harden into a conviction of the demise of pregnant spirit; once that position is reached the next step, for whatever philosophical reasons, becomes the "death of Man" in an age of computer-robots and dread of nuclear technology. (pp. 46–47)

It is because of Harris's deep sense of the fundamental human significance of this question that I am encouraged to ask that he and other critics of world literature written in English take another look at Charlotte Brontë's *Jane Eyre,* which is consistently depreciated when Jean Rhys's *Wide Sargasso Sea* is (justly) appreciated, something which I find too facile. I would strongly urge readers to give their attention to the interpretation in the "monumental" work by Sandra Gilbert and Susan Gubar, *The Madwoman in the Attic: The Woman Writer and the Nineteenth-Century Literary Imagination,*[3] in which, in their chapter on *Jane Eyre,* they document meticulously their reading of Bertha as Jane's double, an avatar of Jane, whose deeds duplicate Jane's anger and dreams, even to the desire to burn down Thornfield Hall, symbol of Rochester's mastery and her own servitude; it is only when Thornfield Hall *is* burnt down and a marriage of equality is possible that Jane can happily enter into a mutual relationship with him, something that Antoinette in Jean Rhys's work might also have found satisfying. Of course Charlotte Brontë does not have Jean Rhys's knowledge of slavery and conquest in the Caribbean nor what Harris refers to as her "imaginative inheritances" both "white" and "black" which link her imagination to Arawak myth through her awareness of Caribbean *obeah,* but neither is it a work to be dismissed as an expression of a rigid view imposed by a partial culture masquerading as totality, at least insofar as the relationship between men and women is concerned. Women's studies in the field of literature have often widened the scope of our understanding of the literary imagination and its role in enriching life, and very often these studies, too, have helped to cross cultural barriers, since what Harris calls the consistent disadvantaging of women cuts across place and time. I feel Gilbert and Gubar's analysis should be studied before critics again dismiss *Jane Eyre* as a work in which Jane and Bertha are intended as polarizations, angel and monster, sanity and madness; Jane's feeling of madness, of wild rebellion and rage and their parallels in Bertha need to be reviewed.

"The Whirling Stone" chapter adds a new dimension to the conception of doubles in literature itself: Harris sees many works as parallels in unsuspected ways, as in the case of *Wide Sargasso Sea* and *The Double Invention of Komo*: "Neither mirrors the other in like rhetoric or appearance, yet a significant likeness exists when one perceives the extremities that live in each work . . . (p. 55). The catholicity of *Wide Sargasso Sea* turns into subtle *coniunctio* of cultures that address the sparked cradle of Komo" (p. 56). Paule Marshall's *The Chosen Place, the Timeless People* parallels works involving a "death of Man" (p. 57) symbol in Harris's view, and he feels that a parallel can be charted to Poe's *Pym*, seeing, as I understand it, an ambivalent rebellion within each work. While her intuitive imagination uses flying and falling motifs running through Icarus, Anancy, and flying trickster folklore and oral African/American traditions of slaves longing for wings to fly home, the novel, on the face of it, presents the "folk body" of an imaginary Caribbean island as so resistant to change as to make the novel seem what Harris calls a "comedy of manners" (p. 68) work of fiction. He feels that she has not pursued the clues her intuitive imagination has expressed that might have opened up the possibility of change. Only "involuntarily" does the novel expose "adventitious 'timeless order' built on terror of the unknown" (p. 59). Nevertheless the "seminal force of arbitrating genius" in this work, as in the others previously examined, "is never entirely vanquished" (p. 61). A potential of dynamic cross-cultural perception resides, Harris seems to be saying, in the intuitive imagination that can lead to change in the inner and outer life of humanity. While it is too late for Poe to consider this, Paule Marshall will find it thought-provoking.

A very important strand in the cultural web Harris weaves in *The Womb of Space* is his interpretation of Patrick White's *Voss* and of what the cross-cultural approach can help us to see better in "another deceptively realistic novel . . . by the great Australian novelist Patrick White" (p. 66). (He has in mind "the realistic texture" of the work that tends to give a common-sense vision to events [p. 69].) He relates *Voss*, throughout the section called "Paradoxes of Form", to the works earlier considered, through its images of pregnancy; mental travel; doubles and shadows; seals on the imagination blocking mutuality; the alchemization of hubris; bridges between day and night; "perpetual discovery"; alchemized stone; expanding circles; "invisible man"; and, finally, the Rainbow Serpent that writes itself with stars in the sky, revealing the death of Voss as "consistent with creation myth rooted in the necessity for community to evolve through complex visions of apparent catastrophe" (p. 76). It is not the apparent realism that fascinates Harris in *Voss* but its "curiously subversive fantasy" (p. 70). The reader of *The Womb of Space*, too, will draw parallels – between White's partial interchange of disadvantaged and privileged lives and Harris's dialogue with otherness; between Harris's "alchemization of hubris" and the thrust in the novel towards this alchemization in the white explorer Voss, who would cut himself off from all "flesh-and-blood contact" (p. 67) with others, who jubilantly saw himself as God, whose "implicit obsession with conquest turns . . . upon him" (p. 77); and between the Rainbow Serpent, "the Great Snake, the grandfather of all men . . . come down from the north in anger" (p. 76) and Harris's "untamable cosmos". And in many other ways the fantasy in *Voss* seems to be closely related to the imagination of Wilson Harris. Both are subversive of divisions in humanity.

In all the works I have mentioned and in those treated in the last two chapters, Harris finds clear sparks of the "intuitive" imagination. Only in regard to *The Serpent and the Rope* by the twentieth-century Indian writer Raja Rao does he find that kind of imagination very much suppressed, though he considers the work an imaginative achievement of a sort, perhaps the most remarkable "and profoundly intelligent example of the combination of Western historical consciousness and non-evolutionary Indian stasis" (p. 78), a combination that he feels characterizes much twentieth-century Indian literature. The discussion (need I say?) shows no animus towards India, nor towards Rao. One gets the impression that Harris wrote this section as a duty, to reveal "patterns of consent" to things as they are, rather than to creative change, to a "seductive passivity" in the face of what is supposedly "the incorrigible pathos of time" (p. 79). The novel's symbols are rooted in the concept of a "timeless order of mind" (p. 78), of "absolute Non-Dual Ego" of "absolute order". Such a philosophy divorces itself from conceptions of "evolutionary marriage between cultures and peoples" (p. 78). God in Hindu theology, Harris tells us, is not "Other" but pre-empts all selves within absolute Non-Dual Ego, subjecting all natures "in concubinage to the Ego" (p. 80), not to a true marriage. "Changeless order . . . is stained by mental incest" (p. 81), says Harris, thus making a connection with *Intruder in the Dust* imagery. These things make Rao's novel "a profoundly revealing, confessional fiction of conservative Southern India. Equally fascinating is the degree to which it resembles European despair and the philosophies of the absurdity of mutual existences or genuine wealth in reciprocity between cultures" (p. 81). What Harris feels is absent is "the conception of psychical re-dress leading into economical or cultural metamorphosis" (p. 81). Harris, however, senses also "remorse and misgiving, if not the torture of the damned" (p. 83) in Rao's book.

The last two lines in *The Womb of Space* are by Whitman and never has Whitman's meaning been more clear to me than in this context: "O you singer solitary, singing by yourself, projecting me, / O solitary me listening, never more shall I cease perpetuating you" (p. 137). American-born Whitman could be saying this to Harris; Guyanese-born Harris could be saying it to Whitman; each of them could be saying it to each of us. That, among a wealth of other things, is what *The Womb of Space: The Cross-Cultural Imagination* conveys.

Chapter 7

The Evolution of Female Figures and Imagery in Wilson Harris's Novels

[T]he shift which is visible in *Invisible Man* is a subtle stroke of genius, and consists in unravelling the masked presence of the female upon or beneath rainbow arcs or bridges between cultures. This, I believe, reveals the bleakness of awakenings black Odysseus experiences when the female is consistently disadvantaged.

    – Wilson Harris, *The Womb of Space: The Cross-Cultural Imagination*

. . . wrapped by influences all tending to make his fancy pregnant with many a mighty birth.

    – Herman Melville, *Moby-Dick*

Men tell her that she is a muse. Yet she knows she is not a muse, she *has* a muse (and what is its sex?).

    – Sandra Gilbert, on problems women poets confront as a result of "male metaphors" and of being mythologized by men, in an essay in the anthology *Poetics: Essays on the Art of Poetry*

[Women] lack that blood congested genital drive which energizes every great style.

    – William Gass's image of the imagination, offered here as a contrast to Melville's and Harris's.

Women and men will be more free and equal after we have re-visioned the concepts of "masculine" and "feminine" essences, "female principle" and "male principle" and understand these not as immortal archetypal ideas but as cultural artefacts.
  – Anonymous

This attempt to focus on female figures and yet not isolate them from the complex "infinite canvas" of the work of Wilson Harris can prove valuable to any significant degree only if it initiates an exchange of views among Harris readers and becomes a shared enterprise. This reader was encouraged to embark on the exploration of this vital subject by Harris's belief, expressed in *The Womb of Space*, that the status of women in fiction, whether it be pre-Columbian myth or modern novel, is crucial to humanity, for where women are undervalued, exploited or degraded, "it is not surprising that ideologies harden into a conviction of the demise of pregnant spirit; once that position is reached the next step, for whatever philosophical reasons, becomes the 'Death of Man' ". My concentration in my reconnaissance, however, was not on Harris's philosophy as such but on the effect upon the reader of his ways of embodying it in his narratives, his "dramas of consciousness". "The reader", of course, can mean only *this* reader, but other dedicated Harris readers, as one sees from the critical literature, share my interpretation of many of the female figures even if not my reaction to them in every instance.

No two Harris novels are alike in their embodying of the idea that all human beings carry within them buried selves, both male and female, of different races, times and places, and the idea that the future depends upon our ability to know these buried selves as part of each of us and of all of us as one humanity whose life or death hangs in the balance in this age. However, there are new developments in the conception of the female characters in *The Angel at the Gate* and *Carnival* that I will treat separately, with special emphasis on *Carnival.* I will consider first the works preceding 1982, then *Angel,* then *Carnival,* and then conclude with a look to a future in the work of Harris that I anticipate with near-certainty and delight.

Powerfully and from his first published novel *Palace of the Peacock* on, the female figures in each work have conveyed the fundamental idea that the disadvantaging of women is destructive to both men and women and that a change is essential to bring about the resurrection of the human creative spirit which alone can preserve the world. The polarization of ideas about women as madonnas or whores, totally rejected by Harris, is a main focus of attention in almost every novel. The image of the womb as the symbol of the imagination (as of other wall-less wombs of time and space) becomes central to Harris's thought in *The Waiting Room* and *Tumatumari*. The latter is the first in which there is a large and varied cast of female characters, the other novels in the pre-1982 period that contain such a cast being *Companions of the Day and Night* and *Da Silva da Silva's Cultivated Wilderness*.

With such contributions to our understanding of a total all-inclusive humanity, and with the continuously implied theme of a cross-cultural imagination that crosses sex boundaries as well as cultural ones, what can there possibly be to question? Yet we have all been affected by traditional notions of non-intrinsic sex differences. (An illustration, expressing an idea never to be expressed again by Harris, indicates that none of us is yet free of some of these ideas. In *Palace* the male I-narrator says, "I was frightened for no reason whatever. The step near me stopped and stood still. I stared around me wildly, in surprise and terror, and my body grew faint and trembling *as a woman's or a child's*."[1] However much women readers of Harris may love children, many are not likely to enjoy this grouping into men on the one hand and women and children on the other.) I wonder mainly about the female figures who are "muses". They are movingly portrayed, the outstanding example being Mariella in *Palace* (youth and age, innocence and guilt), and their significance is much more than that of the usual feminine "muse" in fiction. They embody a folk or a culture, and only when the male to whom they are related in the narrative recognizes them as a necessary part of his inner being is there a hope of rebirth for him and a future for all. But they are more purely symbolic figures than the male characters are, with the exception of Susan in *The Waiting Room* and Prudence in *Tumatumari,* if these are indeed intended to be muses as Hena Maes-Jelinek, Harris's outstanding interpreter, believes. The male characters, though symbolic in one sense, usually seem very much more alive. The muses arouse the imaginations of the male characters but, with the important exceptions just noted, do not seem to have imaginations of their own, although we know from

Harris's philosophy that they must. Nor do they seem in the narratives to have significance outside of their relations with the males, whereas the males always have a being apart from the female characters. They are active in other than their sex-oriented roles, the main male character being captain, engineer, surveyor, explorer, painter or writer. The female characters, muses or not, are seen solely, in the pre-1982 novels, as wives, mistresses or prostitutes and especially as mothers, potential mothers or women unable to be mothers. The most active of the female characters, Magda in *The Whole Armour* and Beti in *The Far Journey of Oudin*, are not muse figures, I think, and only they and the women in *Companions* make decisions and take action on their own. Only in three outstanding novels in the first two decades of Harris's work do the changes in consciousness occur in the female character: Sharon in *The Whole Armour*, Susan in *The Waiting Room* and Prudence in *Tumatumari* — at least in a dramatic way. It is true that in Beti the fact that a development in her has taken place is shown dramatically, but we have not seen the process occurring as is the case with most of Harris's major male characters. One further change should be marked in his fictional work preceding *The Angel at the Gate*. In *The Guyana Quartet* the child whose birth is expected (in the two works in which there is one) is understood to be a son. In *Heartland, Tumatumari* and *Da Silva*, the one expected is simply a child. It should be noted, however, that as far back as Harris's second novel, *The Far Journey of Oudin*, Ram, who has tried to take possession of the expected son of Beti and dead Oudin so that he may have an heir but is defeated by Beti, sees her as the "daughter of a race that was being fashioned anew",[2] though whether he accepts this or will fight it has never been clear to me. In *Companions,* wherein there is an unusual overlapping of male and female characters and characteristics, the child is "the child of humanity", and the long-awaited child of Jen and Da Silva in *Da Silva* and *The Tree of the Sun* may be of either sex. Harris's conception in the latter book is the work of a great poetic genius; I do, however, wonder why Jen, while she is essential to the philosophy of both books in which she appears, plays almost no role in the *narrative* of either, other than to be intrinsic to the artist, as he to her, and to become pregnant with their child. The idea of each living within the other, linking each other to other selves of other times and places, and sharing in each other's creations is exquisitely expressed in what they *say* to each other in the opening scene of *Tree* as in the closing scene in *Da Silva,* but the impression on the reader of the fictional development can be demonstrated by Maes-Jelinek's conclusion in *Wilson Harris* that *he is the artist, she the muse.* Of course, in one sense, Julia, who figures prominently in the narrative, one of the two main characters from the past whom Da Silva paints onto his canvas, is an earlier appearance of Jen – the feminine part of humanity – and in that sense Jen is present throughout, but Da Silva – in his present and also earlier incarnation as the secret novelist Francis – is still the male embodiment of the artist.

The Angel at the Gate brings the most prominent figure, who is female, close to being the creative writer, but there are narrative obstacles in the way of such a perception of her. There are by now several fine summaries and interpretations of the novel (for example, Maes-Jelinek's in *Kunapipi* and Jean-Pierre Durix's in *World Literature Written in English*), so I will confine myself here to the question of why I think Harris divided the writer's role in two, assigning one aspect to Mary and one to W.H., the author of the note that precedes the narrative (at the same time that it is essential to it) and of the book we read in its present form, and to why this reader cannot quite accept Mary's role as equal to that of W.H. or of any fully creative writer, especially in Harris's own terms in his critical essays.

It is my understanding that for Harris the creative process is one "in which the imagination plays a role that is 'passive' as well as active, not imposing itself upon the material . . . freeing itself as completely as possible from its own preconceptions and limitations, and being itself continuously transformed in the experiment".[3] But the *active* role of expressing fictionally the insights gained in this passive, receptive state cannot be denied. Mary, who under the "hypnotic" influence of her "employer" Father Joseph Marsden meets inner selves of other times, places, colours, cultures and conditions, and records these meetings in automatic writing, plays the passive role. W.H., to whom Marsden turns over her dictated notes and who presents them in the book, plays the active role. Mary, the female, conveys, but unconsciously, the dangers of our divided world in an age of the possibility of nuclear war, and our hope, if we achieve the unity of the sacred human family, of preserving humanity. But she is both influenced by and interpreted by an actively creative male. Harris refers to Mrs Yeats, wife of the poet, whose automatic writing came to her from an "unknown writer" who dictated to her. Harris quotes from the back cover of *A Vision*: "Mrs Yeats's efforts at automatic writing led to the conscious formulation of an elaborate system of actively related opposites, providing Yeats with something in which he could finally believe, something that left his 'imagination free to create as it chose'."[4] So *Yeats* is the one with the imagination that creates, though Mrs Yeats is the medium. Nevertheless Mary's consciousness *is* the one in which the drama takes place. It is Marsden's feeling that after his death her diminutive stature will increase "to encompass men and women everywhere in mutual arts of the genius of love" (p. 84). "Perhaps," says W.H., interpreting for him, "his mind was already inching forward into a feminine vessel" (p. 85). Perhaps within Mary and what she symbolizes in union with her inner selves will be the "capacity for conversion of deeds to avert catastrophe" (p. 88). (The foregoing quotation should prove that Harris's concern is with deeds too, not consciousness alone, in our age, the horrors and dangers of which *Angel* presents.) In *Angel* too there is a large and varied cast of female characters, and Jackson, the Jamaican, is at times "almost feminine in spirit" (p. 100). Most significant of all in the evolution of Harris's female figures is the new conception of the twentieth-century "daughter of man" (p. 90) (Jackson's child) to join the old, old conception of the "son of man". This is an eloquent example of Harris's long dedication to a "transformed and transforming tradition". In addition, these children of the family of humanity are of different colours and cultures.

In *Carnival* Harris transforms Dante's "comedy" into a work about "the twentieth-century divine comedy of existence"[5] – its paradoxes and dangers and its need to find a non-violent way to a creative future of peace on the earth which is at once our purgatory and all we know of hell or moments of paradise – the only place we know in the cosmos where humanity can live. As Dante in *The Divine Comedy* searched for the essence of his age through the creation of memorable images, Harris in *Carnival* searches for what is essential in ours through new metaphors, strange at first, then memorable: carnival masks and marble women; waterfalls and rainbow bridges; nebula crabs and Vega; plantation and factory Infernos: cuckold masks and dancing boulders; oracles; those who limp or are in limbo; a burning schooner; pagan Christ; and a ladder to heaven that survives the fire which destroys the building that had contained it – images that can be seen on rereading to be, like "the past and the present and the future [together] *parts* of an unfathomable Carnival whole", beyond "total capture" (p. 31). Images like these, or like the Trojan horse that resembles the womb of a new age, are strange, but the aspects of our lives they seek to penetrate are known to us. Again like Dante, Harris writes here about the main areas of earthly human life in an age on the verge of some great change for good or ill; he continues to seek that "supplement of soul"[6] that we must find in our "deeply troubled violent age". Underwater worlds and outer galaxies are visible, but Harris's response is, at heart, to this world and century.

New Forest (suggested by Dante's dark wood, I should think) is this Harris novel's name for Guyana and, by extension, for the world (as, later in the work, London represents it). New Forest carnival masks are the physical exteriors or roles or conditions everyone bears in period after period; we read of the life or "lives and masks" of Everyman Masters who dies twice between 1917 and 1983 and then returns; in one life he is a plantation overseer who is killed by one of the estate women he has slept with, while later he is an exploited factory worker in London. (One must wonder how much Hindu ideas of reincarnation and universal soul and images of tree and egg influenced the young Wilson Harris in Guyana, a large part of Guyana's population being of Hindu descent.) Harris tries to penetrate the masks of successive ages; the narrator says: "I sought to trace an initial unity of Mankind that was so nebulous it ran through every timepiece of frozen fire one wore on one's wrist (as on the broken body of generations) within fragmented conventions and treaties, false clarities, false economic ideals" (*Carnival*, p. 46).

Everyman Masters is the narrator's guide to Infernos and elsewhere on purgatorial earth; Amaryllis, first seen when she and the narrator (Weyl) meet in the South American interior when they are seven years old and who later is his wife, is the one with whom he glimpses "Paradise" on earth. Masters has brought her back from death and the narrator back from the future via dream and reversible memory, "the future in the past, the past in the future". Besides these participants in the drama there is a very large and heterogeneous cast that includes many doubles, counterparts and twins. Masters's twin, Doubting Thomas, though called a cousin (the name Thomas means twin), is also a guide to Weyl: he symbolizes the doubt the narrator feels is necessary in his attempts to fathom uncertainties; he is "acutely more relevant to me, and my age, than Faith" (p. 33) – a necessary attitude when Faith congeals into a fortress that blocks our vision of the starving and the emaciated in every corner of the globe" (p. 59). It is concern about the plight of this huge population of the world, and about the dangers to humanity in this accident-prone, suicidal age (when "traffic on earth" may cease and there will be no stairway to heaven anywhere in the cosmos) that ceaselessly motivates this extraordinary work of art.

There are innumerable scenes in *Carnival* – beneath the ocean and in space as well as on earth and in fire – and countless characters of both sexes. I can try here only to begin with a few general comments about the female members of the cast and then concentrate on the two that I find most significant in relation to the development of female figures in Harris's novels. In general, the women in *Carnival* suffer as a result of the "false economic ideals" (p. 46) and false standards of our age. The sugar plantation women are exploited economically and sexually. The market woman, strong and outspoken in public, fears her "lover" Johnny, called "the czar", and when he calls her a whore she almost comes to believe she really is the "individual rotten whore that the idiot giant said she was" (p. 66). Masters's mother, pregnant by a man she knows will not marry her, in a layer of New Forest society in which this is a disgrace, almost has an abortion she would not really want, but Masters's true though not biological father marries her to protect her and her child. Weyl's mother, also pregnant, is for the same reason forced to marry Weyl's biological father; although they love each other and would have married anyway, the fact that they were pushed into marriage mars their happiness. (The mother suffers from bouts of depression; the father fears that his son – to whom he feels he has given birth – will be a pawn like his parents, a fate he helps to prevent by a later act of conscience.) And because of an old ritual an Amerindian woman is killed by her son to release her from suffering; he is then put to death by the court of New Forest's civilized and Christian culture that projects its absolutes when judging other cultures. Less appealing females – Charlotte Bartleby who cares about money, not people, and the dancer Aimee in London – have been corrupted by false ideas of power and sex.

Female imagery is especially significant in *Carnival* and is intrinsic to the narrative and its conceptions. In the womb of time the foetus of an age may develop or be aborted; re-entering the womb of time may mean rebirth; even a slight degree of evolution of humanity is new birth. The coitus between men and women that is "totally functional, totally without thought, imagination" (p. 60) is contrasted with "the innermost spirit of Sex, the spirit of brooding creativity that takes over where nature leaves off" (p. 30) and is the "capacity to set material pride aside in favour of the spirit of care". In the characters, scenes and relationships in the narrative these general metaphors are given concrete expression in human form throughout. One female figure, whom I have hesitated to call a character, is pure spirit in human form: the young "immortal" (p. 82) Alice whose dance is "the dance of sublimity" (p. 82) and who expresses the "spirit of a body" (p. 83) ("half sleeping, half leaping" [p. 83] between heaven and earth) as she jumps over higher and higher bars.

Old Alice Bartleby has lived in the Alms House "for ten years or fifteen ages" and is called Aunt by all. She seems at first a minor character, but her reappearance in the narrative at the end gives her role a major significance. Her last name is the same as that of Melville's Bartleby: "No relation, I hasten to say, to Herman Melville's Bartleby, though fiction-spirit, fiction-blood runs between them" (p. 39). There is "a family tree of spirit" (p. 41), the narrator says, and this unites not only Aunt Alice and Bartleby, both seemingly condemned to oblivion, but also Harris and Melville. Elsewhere Harris has explained that in her case the seeming oblivion is transformed by the spirit of love that dwells in her despite the "horrendous poverty of the colonial civilization in which she lives. That seed – the seed of the genius of love – begins to indicate the evolution of a twentieth-century *purgatorio* and *paradiso* from within limbo itself."[7] Though Melville's male Bartleby has become Alice Bartleby, Harris's imagination in our age has invested her with "the seed of the genius of love" not present in Melville's Bartleby. This does not mean that Harris feels this genius resides only in women; elsewhere in *Carnival* he speaks of "the androgyny of the heart" and in the letter quoted above says that in *all* characterization by a writer of fiction there are "buried male and female elements".[8] (I find it impossible to think in terms of separate male and female elements of character rather than simply of human elements. It is the human element that *Carnival* as a whole dramatizes, the idea of one humanity in one linked chain of existences from one generation to another and crossing cultural and gender lines.)

Towards the end of the novel, when Aunt Alice Bartleby leans down from the "bars of heaven" (p. 143) to warn Masters (accompanied by Weyl) of danger, she assumes her crucial role in the narrative, symbolizing the love and human concern — despite the hard life she has had — that brings the narrator to hear and clearly understand his deceased lawyer father's defence years earlier of the young Amerindian matricide who was condemned to death for obeying his "pagan" ritual. Harris implies that it is necessary to penetrate the "pagan womb from which we all derive" (pp. 103–4), to understand without condemnation what frozen ritual leads to, for ours surely is a world of ritual violence on the largest scale. Weyl now says of his father, who was broken on the wheel because of his unconventional act of defending the young matricide, "My father had defended a pagan El Doradan whose hideous imperatives could be traced far up, far back, into ancient fires when statesmen-priests broke the organ in their victim's chest and offered it to the sun – or should the sun fail – to unknown fires far out in space, to foetal planets around Vega" (p. 142). Alice Bartleby's genius of love has helped bring the son closer to the father, the present closer to the past, one culture closer to another and to an understanding of the need for creative change if we would not condemn future children to extinction because of our own hideous imperatives. She instructs Masters to turn back to archaic Earth that still needs him to help wed partial things to each other (as he "weds" Weyl and Amaryllis). Aunt Alice is concerned because of her "universal . . . kinship to humanity" (p. 40). We now know why her curious dance was early in the narrative said to symbolize the "thirst for proof of genuine survival" (p. 41), why she is called Aunt by Harris, and why she is presented as a "mystery that runs far deeper than proof or parody of the evolution of limbo into heaven" (p. 42).

The last of Harris's female figures so far is Amaryllis, whose voice is the last we hear in *Carnival*. (It may be that her name was suggested by Virgil's shepherdess since Virgil was Dante's guide. It may have had special appeal because it is the name of a flower that, if it is cared for, blooms year after year – is resurrected, if we use the metaphor that stands out towards the end of *Carnival*.) Once Amaryllis enters the drama, she and the narrator seem truly to be one human being in two interrelating parts, each with corresponding buried selves to share with the other. They are opposites only in the sense of being fulfilling opposites necessary to true life, as contrasted with dead existences. And while the child they will love is not physically their own, it is – in the sense of care for the future – truly and equally theirs. And this child, symbolizing the future, is female. "Should she," says Weyl, "survive into a new century of mind we may all recover" (p. 171). Weyl's father had felt himself a pawn; Weyl, the narrator, feels himself now half-puppet, half-human; this female child, if she is allowed to survive in this atomic age, will be more human than either.

This birth, however, occurs in 1983 ("or is it 2083?"). It is in 1958 that Amaryllis, whom the narrator has brought back from the underworld in a transformed version of the Orpheus myth (she would return with him whether he looked back or looked forward) is united with the narrator in a true marriage presided over by Spirit, not a priest or an official of the state. A symbolic scene that unites their spiritual and physical love and unites also basic themes of the book leads to that perception through the senses yet "beyond" them that is a unique achievement of Harris's poetic art.

The "love scene" occurs in autumn, a year before their legal marriage. Amaryllis's bedroom atop a building overlooking misty Regent's Canal in London is spacious, and a fire blazes in the grate creating the "illusion" of mist and space. Note in the passage that follows the continuous use of the word "we" in describing sensations of lovemaking, another unique fictional phenomenon:

> That fire . . . had achieved the miracle of a flower in which we perceived the mystery
> of . . . the first seed eaten by revolutionary spirit ages ago, the first leaf phantom god

(phantom animal) tasted, the first plant upon the tongue of the sea, the first rose in the lips of soil. We were drowning together in fire and in water, the strangest taste of dying into elements we consumed, the strangest climax, reality of paradise, reality of intercourse; inimitably transparent yet dense bodies were ours. We lived in yet out of our frames, we touched each other yet were free of possession, we embraced yet were beyond the net of greed, we were penetrated yet whole, closer together than we had ever been yet invisibly apart. We were ageless dream . . . In the fire and in the flower, in the rain of autumn leaves that the cosmic horse eats, lies the thrust of revolutionary peace within two beings alone, yet encompassed by an invisible third, an invisible fourth, an invisible fifth, sixth, seventh, in the belly of space, the invisible army of humanity. (pp. 123–24)

The narrator thinks of their freedom to love each other (though different in skin colour), and the thought makes him think of South Africa and he feels that his freedom, which is only partial, interlinks him with others who are in chains and makes him responsible to make vows to them as to Amaryllis.

The last scene occurs in 1983 (or 2083). The narrator and Amaryllis are in Addison Road in London, where they live in an "ocean wave" (p. 169). Weyl knows that he has seen the last of Masters. Amaryllis sits beside him with the girl child they will care for in her arms. They know who the Christian mother is, and Masters, whom the narrator has related to "pagan Christ", may be the father. To Weyl this would be the happiest of coincidences. Such a blend, he feels, would illumine and redeem the "global meaninglessness" that stems from fear of those who are of other cultures, the fear that "threatens all, that threatens to abort submarine as well as superstellar civilization" (p. 171).

The voice of Amaryllis ends the work in what is more of an artistic closure than is usual in a Harris novel:

Whether she is Masters' child or not, she runs in parallel with all wasted lives to be redeemed in time. And in that spirit she is his child. She is our child . . . *The love that moves the sun and the other stars* moves us now, my dearest husband, my dearest Jonathan, to respond with originality to each other's carnival seas of innocence and guilt, each other's Carnival lands of subterfuge and truth, and each other's Carnival skies of blindness and vision. (pp. 171–72)

Early in *Carnival* the narrator had said that he and other "character-masks" were the joint authors of Carnival and he was in a sense their creation. Masters had conferred upon him the responsibility of "spirit-parent . . . fiction-maker" (p. 31). Relating this idea to Harris and Amaryllis, we can say that while he has been creating her, she has been re-creating him. He has conceived her as intelligent, loving, responsible to humanity of all time, and as convincingly half of the male narrator; *and she has a voice; she has ideas.* So there are signs in *Carnival – and* in *The Angel at the Gate,* though to a lesser extent – that in a Harris work of the near future a creative artist in female form will come to birth, signs that the fictional male writer/artist of his novels has been secreting a fictional female creative artist with pen or paintbrush in hand.

Chapter 8

Wilson Harris's Cross-Cultural Dialogue with Melville

Despite his having written twenty novels, all published by Faber and Faber, one critical work published here by Greenwood Press, extraordinary poetry and philosophical and critical essays; in spite of his being described as "Certainly the greatest novelist writing in the English language today" (Kathleen Raine, poet and Blake scholar of international reputation whose books have been translated into many languages) and as the writer whose novels will be read fifty years from now (Robert Nye, British critic); and even though he has been visiting professor at Yale, University of Texas at Austin, University of California at Santa Cruz and speaker at other campuses as California Regents fellow, as well as elsewhere in the United States, a very small number of people in our country are familiar with Wilson Harris's work or even name. True, in 1973 he and Achebe were the subject of a week-long conference at the University of Missouri, which was made possible by the National Endowment for the Humanities. Since 1974 he has been nominated annually for the Nobel prize. His novels have been translated into six languages. Two books about him have been published in the United States, one by Greenwood Press and one by G.K. Hall, listed in the material I have distributed.

What threads in his life can remind us of Melville? Melville was born in 1819 in a city once called New Amsterdam. Harris was born in 1921 in another New Amsterdam, a small village on the east coast of Guyana, the only English-speaking country in South America, on the northeast shoulder of the continent, in many, but not all, ways a Caribbean country. The largest part of the population is descended from indentured servants from India who were brought to the plantations when slavery ended and those of African descent left for the towns or established villages of their own. Other indentured workers brought there from China (only men) and workers who came from Portugal did not satisfy the planters, and the Amerindians would not leave the interior. Many Guyanese today are of mixed origins, racial, geographic or religious. Several origins are, especially in the capital, often incorporated in the same person. Wilson Harris is descended from European, African and Amerindian forbears. ("Amerindian" is the word used in that part of the world to describe the original people of the land.)

The striking and significant parallel in Melville's and Harris's personal experience is that both lived for a number of imagination-forming years outside modern civilization, Melville as a sailor and Harris first as assistant and then as chief government surveyor in the interior of Guyana, a territory of jungles, rivers and waterfalls, Kaieteur Falls among them.

Both Melville and Harris came into contact with an original and so-called primitive people and learned from them. But neither is a primitivist: the native peoples in the South Pacific became for Melville a point of reference from which to see the savagery of the nineteenth-century colonialist world, and the Amerindians, who remained outside organized Guyanese society, became for Harris a symbol of all those who have been ignored in life, wiped out in recorded history and dimmed in our imaginations – an example of the obscure person through whose eyes we should strive to see, and of a past with which we must enter into a new relationship for a necessary renewal of forgotten sympathies and a new conception of humanity and community – one of the many peoples in the world whom Harris sees as part of our own buried selves.

These experiences of Melville at sea and Harris in the interior of his country and self provided symbols that were to be essential elements of each one's unique vision of the world. They see things similarly in many ways, differently in others, reflecting, in large part, the expanding scientific changes in the world and the deepening of the crises confronting us today. But, while their imaginations lead them on different paths, they conceive of the poetic imagination similarly: Harris's critical book in the series edited by John Blassingame and Henry Louis Gates, Jr, is called *The Womb of Space: The Cross-Cultural Imagination;* Melville, too, conceives of the imagination as a womb. As a whaleman he had been, like the mixed crew of whalemen, "wrapped by influences all tending to make his fancy pregnant with many a mighty birth".[1] Of course there are fundamental differences. Melville's art presents vivid, *indelible* images symbolizing aspects of the world. In Harris's novels each unforgettable scene is a dissolving part of a "web of processes"[2] in which all is crumbling and reintegrating in each impossible-to-isolate moment; a single Harris image is likely to go through an evolutionary process; its implications change from context to context until in the end they may be quite different from what they started out to be. Finally in this introduction to Harris, I would like to point out that Melville has been from the start one of the great writers to whom Harris responds – along with Homer, Dante, Blake, Eliot and the now unknown makers of myths. In lectures he has been giving at British universities this year, he links Sophocles in *Antigone,* Dante in *The Divine Comedy,* and Melville and Malcolm Lowry in his discussion of allegory. Each in his day, Melville from *Mardi* on, and Harris from the start, has been considered a very difficult writer. I hasten to add that each has an irrepressible sense of humour.

Both Melville and Harris feel a deep desire for a community of imagination. Melville hoped to find it in Hawthorne. Harris's central passion is for a "deep-seated, mutual, cross-cultural dialogue between imaginations",[3] of many times and places, whether expressed in the great classics or in folk literature and myth, Calypso songs, or literature from Greece, Rome, Africa or wherever. These references do not mean influences, but that "drawn backwards and forwards into other imaginations"[4] of the past, present or possible future, he, like Melville, takes what seizes him as suggestive, finding something in the fabric of another text and re-visioning its implications. To Harris tradition is something continually transformed and transforming.

I do not know whether Harris was thinking of *Moby-Dick* when he wrote *Palace of the Peacock,* but, while different, there is a kinship between the two. These links were noted early by Ivan van Sertima and C.L.R. James. And Harris early listed Melville first among his examples of native/universal artists engaged in the re-creation of the epic, which in his mind deals with the "soul" and hidden unity of humanity, a form that appears, disappears and reappears unevenly, and in a new shape with new implications, part of the cross-cultural dialogue between imaginations of the writer's time and his or her past and future. Of the need for a new kind of "heterogeneous" novel to focus on humanity rather than on supposedly sovereign individual men and women, he finds that "one would have to turn to Melville to find the beginning of this kind of thing in the novel".[5] He feels, too, that nineteenth-century Melville brought the novel "to a frontier he did not cross but that needed to be crossed; herein lies his profound genius".[6] Melville pushed forward the threshold of art and thought in that time, turning away from the "authoritarian story line" and the bare realism prevailing in his day.

Now, in the 1990s, Harris expresses the way in which he finds himself rereading certain novels. He starts with *Moby-Dick,* as reread in the light of an allegory of an abyss that may not be an abyss. He changes Gertrude Stein's "A rose is a rose is a rose" into "An abyss is an abyss is not an abyss."[7] As he reads *Moby-Dick,* Ahab descends into the *inferno* of the abyss. Ishmael is on the same ship, but his turning away from what Melville called the "devil's chase" leads to his being borne up by Queequeg's coffin – "an intuitive confluence of the *inferno* and the *paradiso*"[8] – a strange new way of envisioning *Moby-Dick* as carrying on and revising this tradition. Harris's interpretation implies that Melville deeply sensed this tradition, that it was Melville's intuitive expression of something deep in the human imagination that led him to have Ishmael borne up by the coffin to which he clings at the end. Melville makes "a profound distinction" between Ahab-like activity, his self-preoccupied ambition, and Ishmael's "inner movement towards otherness, inner communion with otherness".[9]

Harris's response to *Bartleby* is expressed in both essay and fiction. The essay "The Fabric of the Imagination" sees Melville's story as "a subtle repudiation of the vocabulary of fate in his age. . . . Bartleby refuses to toe the line and sinks by degrees into a silence that promises to disrupt the frame in which he is set."[10] It is "a pregnant silence that Bartleby nurses" (p. 178), a refusal to participate in his wall-like society, to adhere to block-like, institutional habit. He is found dead in the Tombs, like a huddled foetus at the base of a wall, on turf, where, Melville says, "by some strange magic, through the clefts, grass seed, dropped by birds, had sprung".[11] Harris's response to the final note saying that Bartleby once worked in the dead letter office is to link the grass seed and the letters never delivered. To him the seed grows into a blade of grass, a diminutive pole against which the dead letters may be stacked by Bartleby, bringing non-existent families into being. Bartleby may now surrender himself to otherness and see "into the heart of an *unfinished genesis* of the imagination which he must share with men and women in all future ages, lands, islands, continents" (p. 180). He has resisted being part of his civilization and its values. Melville may have felt that Bartleby's resistance, and his own, carried the seed of something genuinely different. Harris elsewhere refers to Bartleby's pregnant silence, the "seed" idea again. In the novel, *Carnival,* Bartleby "metamorphoses" into a woman called Alice Bartleby who lives in an almshouse in Georgetown in what was then British Guiana. She embodies a barren colonial age. That is "her abyss, her non-existence, so to speak" (p. 180). Her eyes weep for humankind. The essay explains that she is "the mystery of genius within the most unpropitious . . . circumstances" (p. 180). Both male and female Bartleby imply to Harris the need for changes in the ritual habit of a culture and of heart and mind.

In *Carnival,* the novel, Alice Bartleby has lived in an almshouse for "ten years or fifteen or ages".[12] She is related to Melville's Bartleby in the sense that "fiction-spirit, fiction-blood, runs between them" (p. 39). Alice Bartleby's seeming oblivion is transformed by the spirit of love that dwells in her despite the horrendous poverty of the colonial civilization in which she lives. That seed, the seed of the genius of love, begins to indicate "the evolution of a twentieth century *purgatorio* and *paradiso* from within limbo".[13] Harris conceives in *Carnival* a modern allegory in which the inferno, purgatorio and paradiso are overlapping. Towards the end of the novel Alice Bartleby leans down from the "bars of heaven" (p. 143) and brings the narrator to an understanding of his father's legal defence of a young Amerindian matricide whose mother had been deathly ill and suffering and who was condemned to death by the dominant society for obeying his "pagan ritual". Harris speaks of the "pagan womb" from which we all derive (p. 103) and of *our* pagan rituals and ritual violence which may condemn future children to extinction. Melville's Bartleby has entered the womb of space (the cross-cultural imagination uniting times and places) and Harris's Alice Bartleby whose love and understanding are timeless and universal has come to birth. If this all seems out of harmony with Melville's social concerns, I have misled you. Harris is more than aware of every major problem facing us in our age and every major development in the sciences; it is simply that he puts today into a concept of past and future that has no stark boundaries of either time or place.

What Harris does in his essay on *Benito Cereno* is place himself inside the American Captain Delano who comes on board the slave transportation ship, *San Dominick,* and fails to see that the Africans are in control, since he is easily deceived by the masquerade Babo directs, which makes all on the ship appear what he finds "normal". To Harris, looking from within Delano, blacks are faceless, fit only to serve whites; these are Delano's inbuilt "crutches of familiarity".[14] That is why when he sees the ship from a distance he assumes the dark figures moving freely on deck seem black friars. "I am oppressed," says Harris/Delano by "a blanket of value-codes" (p. 47), "fossil value-codes" (p. 49). And why, Harris asks, should Harris/Delano not take it for granted that it is Benito Cereno who is in command and Babo his personal attendant? How could I/he doubt that in Cereno is lodged a dictatorship that, as Melville says, transforms the man into a "block" (p. 56). Is Cereno not the captain? Harris, back in his own person, stresses the static character of a world with this concentration of power. "It is the echo of the objective masquerade, which prefers to arm itself ceaselessly in its submission to death rather than to conceive life by degrees of digestion of the shocks of change that comes home to me, I find, on several levels of *Benito Cereno*" (p. 57). After Babo's execution in Lima and the placing of his head on a pole in the Plaza, twin image as I see it of the skeleton as figurehead, the escalation of relationships, Harris says "breeds a further polarization between an age and eternity . . . The silent crutches of an age" (p. 57) march forward. He feels that at a time when the actors in a civilization become robots of fate, "the irony of comedy [he uses this word as Dante does] lies with the intuitive imagination and how it employs what is apparently evanescent as the writing of the future on the wall of the past" (p. 57). I see a connection with Melville's concept of a wall in *Bartleby*, as I see a link between Melville's "block" and Harris's character named Block in a scene in his novel *Tumatumari*. But in that novel an eye does open in a rock and the gorgon's head flowers.

To many critics *The Confidence-Man* is a "nihilistic moral allegory, sometimes seemingly benevolent". But to Harris, with his sense of the complex potentialities of the trickster, the work reflects the "historical prison" in which Melville lived and "his attempt to forge a 'trickster' gateway between the lie and truth of community".[15] That Melville was trying to find this kind of gateway may, I think, be implied by the possibly half-hopeful last sentence, "Something may follow of this masquerade."[16] Harris says, "Melville's *Confidence-Man* . . . stops upon a frontier of grave uncertainty on one hand and darkened potential on the other."[17] The guises of the confidence man are his many selves which suggest the "otherness of selves within the self".

Of *Billy Budd* Harris thinks, as have others, that the supreme irony of the fixation of authority in Captain Vere is revealed in the execution scene, where, to me, the "block" idea enters again, as Vere stands rigid as a musket in the ship-armourer's rack. But Harris adds a new interpretation of Billy, seen by Vere as an angel of God. Harris emphasizes Billy's response to Claggart's charge against him, saying that such automatic reflex violence, which distinguishes so many societies around the world, is made all the more "terrifying when the 'angel' himself is chained to a convention that eclipses . . . the word".[18]

There are Melville works that have not yet addressed themselves to Harris. It would be interesting to hear his response to *Mardi* in which Taji leaves the ship Arcturion where "days are like cycles in space".[19] He travels through space until he reaches the "great globe of globes" of the mid-nineteenth century, kills to get what he wants, learns nothing that alters him or his outlook, and returns in deliberate death to the "outer ocean". Will this incarnation of nineteenth-century man change in some future one? In regard to *Mardi*, how would Harris respond to Lombardo, author of a *Mardi*-like novel in that it is considered to be wild, unconnected, all episode, who plunges deeper and deeper into himself until a new world does emerge from primal chaos. The characters who are walking about in him at last step forward. He says, "We are full of ghosts; we are graveyards full of buried dead that start to life before us", an idea in harmony with Harris's philosophy. In *Mardi* Melville's view of his world and its relation to the future can be perceived. There is the intimation that a seed of brotherhood and peace in humanity's heart could someday germinate. But will it? The first page of this highly experimental novel asks, "But whence and whither wend ye, mariners?"[20] In the Harris–Melville dialogue across time and cultures, Melville would echo Harris's wish for a seed of genuine hope in a nihilistic and materialistic age characterized by Taji-like individualism and withdrawal from community. And it would be interesting, to hear Harris's response to *The Encantadas,* in particular to the account of the Chola widow, a symbol of suffering humanity, a kind of Christ figure, but female, with both Amerindian and Spanish ancestors.

The dialogue I have sketchily traced reflects in part how the great genius who died a century ago is understood by the one many around the world see as the rare genius of the twentieth. What will the great imaginative writers of future generations say in dialogue with them both?

American students had to wait more than seventy-five years before Melville was accepted into the canon and, in fact, as late as 1940 in the college I attended, English majors were required to take, almost exclusively, courses about British literature. American literature courses were electives and there were very few.

Today, in other countries, Wilson Harris's novels, especially *Palace of the Peacock,* are the subject of university courses, but rarely in our country, even though most university libraries purchase them and more than a few scholars know his work. Will it have to be another seventy-five years before our students in general have the opportunity to have the pleasure and challenge of his work? I use his name here as a symbol of all the newly discovered writers of the past and of the truly creative imaginative writers of the present – and future. What is very strange about the resistance to canon transformation is the failure to see that the development of the human imagination does not suddenly cease.

I close with a quotation from Harris's novel *The Infinite Rehearsal*: "We have a debt to tradition that we need to sight and weave a thread that runs back into the past as it moves into the cross-cultural humanities of the future."[21]

Chapter 9

Wilson Harris
An Introduction

Harris has done so much to unblock the Western mind-set. But even now genius is not totally inhibited by all the counter-forces of the world in crisis. Harris may be one sign of a changing wind.

    – Kathleen Raine

All generations are blended: and heaven and earth of one kin . . . the nations and families, flocks and folds of the earth. . . . All things form one whole.

    – Herman Melville, *Mardi*

The whole crew was one spiritual family living and dying together in a common grave out of which they had sprung again from the same soul and womb as it were.

    – Wilson Harris, *Palace of the Peacock*

Wilson Harris is usually described as a Caribbean writer. He should also be thought of as a South American writer. His early years leading government surveys in the interior of Guyana and his contact with the Amerindians – their culture, myths and condition of being forgotten by the dominant culture – deepened his imagination and concern about all those nameless people in South America who, since the period of the conquistadores, have remained lost in written history. But, above all, Harris has to be thought of as a universal writer, not only because of his concern for all women and men of all times and places but because his imagination plunges into the depths of the earth and also out into the universe. His implied question is: Why must we build bridges between cultures, times, places, earth and space? Our day is filled with potentialities for a totally destructive human future or a truly creative one. His Christ figures may be of pre-Christian times or non-Christian cultures of any time or land. He speaks of the pagan past from which we all have come. His novels may be set in places other than Guyana, but wherever they are set, Harris has all of us in mind. He has hope that humanity will begin to change and re-create itself. Humanity in his fiction is "at the crossroads".

Although Harris's work gives evidence of enormous reading of the work of others, it is fundamentally unlike that of anyone else. Awakening the imagination of his readers beyond its usual limits, he challenges us to think in entirely new ways. His style – if we can consider anything so honest a "style" – is sometimes breathtaking, uniting all the arts and senses, some-times bare or scientific. At times there are abrupt and, for a while, puzzling narrative switches. His recent works contain many "analytical dialogues", as Hena Maes-Jelinek calls them. This is true of the passage from *Jonestown,* his new novel, included in this issue. Harris conceives of his novels as epics, a form he believes need not be lost in a remote past. Some critics have divid-ed Harris's work into periods. To me it has always seemed to be one contin-uing and growing work, never possible to complete. Other critics today think so as well, although Harris's style has changed and his philosophy has become more probing. The reader of Harris's work cannot drift tranquilly along with the narrative. Every word is necessary, almost all are resonant in their suggestiveness. Symbols, charged with new or enriched meanings, reap-pear. Since each character represents the potentialities of humanity, we who read are participants in the narrative and the thought/feeling of the work.

So Harris's novels need to be read with utter attention. His is an integrat-ed imagery of the arts and sciences. The appeal is to the whole person – inner, outer, mind, heart, "soul" – and to aspects of ourselves of which we are unaware. That is why the novels take the form of dreams, dreams being freer than conventional thinking and feeling. Harris's sense of time – of the past alive in the present and of the seeds of the future in both – is central. Most of his characters have names from the past or are symbolic – for example, Penelope, Amaryllis, Poseidon, Faust, Bone, Hope, Abram – but their nature has changed to show the negative and positive potentialities of humanity. The implied question is: Which of these will we develop for a changed future? The creative or the destructive? Harris calls his opus a comedy. Although he does have an irrepressible sense of humour, his use of comedy resembles Dante's in *The Divine Comedy*. All the characters, representing humanity, are dead. When they are "resurrected", how will they (we) think, feel, act? None of the characters represents a static extreme of good or evil. In the unforeseeable future things may be different. For example, a representative character, the female Emma, may become archbishop. If there are no true changes, the human race will end – all possibility of resurrection gone. But Harris retains his hope that we will fundamentally change in time, that the "soul", by which he means the hidden unity of humanity, will prevail.

Harris's introduction to literature began when, as a small child, he found books in his dead father's trunk and his mother taught him to read from them. (His introduction to the *Odyssey* came at that early age.) He was later to read them anew and reinterpret them in his own revisionary imagination, investing them with new significance for our crucial time. To help us see differently, unusual things happen: there are marriages between people not only of different places but of different times; people other than he are the writers of the novels – or are they other people within him?

Experiences in life that impressed him deeply have given his novels their startling titles and symbolism, as exemplified by *Palace of the Peacock, The Four Banks of the River of Space* and *Resurrection at Sorrow Hill*. His sensitivity to the oneness of human life, past and present, and to our environment stems from the years in the rainforests and his dialogues with nature. He questions the rocks whose markings tell of their past, mountain ranges that give evidence of the time when they were under oceans, rivers that relate where they have been and why their paths have changed – all giving answers presenting new mysteries. At the centre of it all is "the frail heartbeat" of humankind.[1]

At the age of thirty-eight, Harris left what was at that time British Guiana to go to London. He has lived for more than thirty years in the United Kingdom. He and his poet and playwright wife Margaret, born in Scotland, live in Essex. They have travelled extensively since his first novel, *Palace of the Peacock,* was published in the 1960s. Besides his twenty novels, all put out by Faber and Faber, he has written much poetry, one short play, numerous critical essays, the texts of talks abroad and a long book of criticism published by Greenwood Press, *The Womb of Space: The Cross-Cultural Imagination.* (Note: the word *cross-cultural* implying bridges between cultures; the word *multicultural* often implies treating cultures as unbridged islands.) This theme is the main emphasis in his work. He has been invited to speak and has taught briefly in many parts of the world. In 1992 he received Italy's Mondello prize for fiction. He has been awarded Guyana's main literature prize. In the United States he has lectured at Yale, the Universities of Buffalo, Texas and Iowa, among others, and he has been a California Regents professor.

Wilson Harris, like Melville, can be viewed from apparently endlessly different angles. The essays here are different and yet enrich each other. They are part of the ongoing project of opening up the work of this most universal and most human of authors.

Notes

Chapter 1

1. Wilson Harris, "The Palace of the Peacock", *Guyana Quartet* (London: Faber and Faber, 1985), 39. Subsequent references appear parenthetically in the text.
2. Wilson Harris, "The Far Journey of Oudin", *Guyana Quartet* (London: Faber and Faber, 1985), 216. Subsequent references appear parenthetically in the text.
3. Wilson Harris, "The Whole Armour", *Guyana Quartet* (London: Faber and Faber, 1985), 333. Subsequent references appear parenthetically in the text.
4. Wilson Harris, "The Secret Ladder", *Guyana Quartet* (London: Faber and Faber, 1985), 464. Subsequent references appear parenthetically in the text.
5. Wilson Harris, *Heartland* (London: Faber and Faber, 1964). Subsequent references appear parenthetically in the text.
6. Wilson Harris, *The Eye of the Scarecrow* (London: Faber and Faber, 1965), 101. Subsequent references appear parenthetically in the text.

Chapter 2

1. Wilson Harris, *Tradition, the Writer and Society: Critical Essays* (London: New Beacon Publications, 1967), 3. Subsequent references appear parenthetically in the text.
2. Wilson Harris, *The Waiting Room* (London: Faber and Faber, 1967). Subsequent references appear parenthetically in the text.

Chapter 3

1. Wilson Harris, *Tumatamari* (London: Faber and Faber, 1968). Subsequent references appear parenthetically in the text.
2. Louis De Broglie, *Physics and Microphysics* (New York: Harper, 1960), 264.

Chapter 4

1. Wilson Harris, *Ascent to Omai* (London: Faber and Faber, 1970), 96. Subsequent references appear parenthetically in the text.

2. Wilson Harris, "The Far Journey of Oudin", *Guyana Quartet* (London: Faber and Faber, 1985), 98.

3. Wilson Harris, *Tumatumari* (London: Faber and Faber, 1968), 89. Subsequent references appear parenthetically in the text.

4. Wilson Harris, *Black Marsden* (London: Faber and Faber, 1972), 104. Subsequent references appear parenthetically in the text.

5. Wilson Harris, *Tradition, the Writer and Society: Critical Essays* (London: New Beacon Publications, 1967), 57. Subsequent references appear parenthetically in the text.

6. Ibid., 32–33; Wilson Harris, *The Eye of the Scarecrow* (London: Faber and Faber, 1965), 50.

7. Jacques Monod, *Chance and Necessity* (New York: Knopf, 1971), xi.

8. Wilson Harris, *The Waiting Room* (London: Faber and Faber, 1967), 67. Subsequent references appear parenthetically in the text.

9. Wilson Harris, *Eternity to Season* (London: New Beacon Books, 1978), 35.

10. J.D. Bernal, *Science in History*, vol. 2 (New York: Cameron Associates, 2d ed., 1956), 30.

11. Werner Heisenberg, *Physics and Beyond: Encounters and Conversations* (New York: Harper and Row, 1971), 164.

12. Wilson Harris, "The Palace of the Peacock", *Guyana Quartet* (London: Faber and Faber, 1985), 134. Subsequent references appear parenthetically in the text.

13. Wilson Harris, *The Age of the Rainmakers* (London: Faber and Faber, 1971), 82.

Chapter 5

1. Ivan van Sertima, "The Sleeping Rocks" (paper presented at the University of Missouri–Kansas City, 21 June 1973).

2. Wilson Harris, in *Kas-kas: Interviews with Three Caribbean Writers in Texas – George Lamming, C.L.R. James, Wilson Harris,* ed. Ian Munro and Reinhard Sander (Austin: African and Afro-American Research Institute, University of Texas at Austin, 1972), 54.

3. Wilson Harris, "A Talk on the Subjective Imagination", *New Letters* (Fall 1973), 42.

4. Herman Melville, *Pierre, or the Ambiguities* (1852; reprint, New York: Hendricks House, 1962), 305.

5. Wilson Harris, *Tradition, the Writer and Society: Critical Essays* (London: New Beacon Publications, 1967), 20.

6. Ibid., 17.

7. Herman Melville, *Moby-Dick, or the Whale* (1851; reprint, New York: Random House, 1930), 821.

8. Ibid., epilogue.

9. Wilson Harris, "The Palace of the Peacock", *Guyana Quartet* (London: Faber and Faber, 1985), 112–13.

10. Ibid., 117.

11. Wilson Harris, *Black Marsden* (London: Faber and Faber, 1972), 11.

12. Ibid., 39.

13. Harris, *Tradition, the Writer and Society,* 8.

Chapter 6

1. John W. Blassingame and Henry Louis Gates, Jr, foreword to Wilson Harris, *The Womb of Space: The Cross-Cultural Imagination* (Westport, Conn.: Greenwood Press, 1983), xii.

2. Wilson Harris, *The Womb of Space: The Cross-Cultural Imagination* (Westport, Conn.: Greenwood Press, 1983), xv. Subsequent references appear parenthetically in the text.

3. Wilson Harris, *Tradition, the Writer and Society: Critical Essays* (London: New Beacon Publications, 1967), 4.

4. Sandra Gilbert and Susan Gubar, *The Madwoman in the Attic: The Woman Writer and the Nineteenth-Century Literary Imagination,* 2d ed. (New Haven: Yale University Press, 2000).

Chapter 7

1. Wilson Harris, "The Palace of the Peacock", *Guyana Quartet* (London: Faber and Faber, 1985), 29.

2. Wilson Harris, "The Far Journey of Oudin", *Guyana Quartet* (London: Faber and Faber, 1985), 238.

3. Joyce Sparer Adler, "*Tumatumari* and the Imagination of Wilson Harris", *Journal of Commonwealth Literature* (July 1969).

4. Wilson Harris, *The Angel at the Gate* (London: Faber and Faber, 1982), 107. Subsequent references appear parenthetically in the text.

5. Wilson Harris, *Carnival* (London: Faber and Faber, 1985), 43. Subsequent references appear parenthetically in the text.

6. Louis De Broglie, "Dawn of the Atomic Age", *Physics and Microphysics* (New York: Harper, 1960), 264.

7. From a letter from Wilson Harris to Joyce Sparer Adler, written in connection with the Melville Society, February 1985, in which Harris speaks also about how a fictional male character created in one culture may secrete a fictional female who will appear in a later culture.

8. Ibid.

Chapter 8

1. Herman Melville, *Moby-Dick, or the Whale* (1851; reprint, New York: Random House, 1930), 260.

2. Wilson Harris, *The Waiting Room* (London: Faber and Faber, 1967), 67.

3. Wilson Harris, "Comedy and Modern Allegory: A Personal View", in *A Shaping of Connections,* edited by Hena Maes-Jelinek, Kersten Holst Petersen and Anna Rutherford (Coventry: Dangaroo Press, 1989), 128.

4. Wilson Harris, "The Radical Imagination", *Lectures and Talks* (Liege: Département d'Anglais, Université de Liège, 1992), 35.

5. Wilson Harris, "A Talk on the Subjective Imagination", *New Letters* (Fall 1973), 42.

6. Private notes of conversation between Wilson Harris and Joyce Sparer Adler, n.d.

7. Harris, "Comedy and Modern Allegory", 130.

8. Ibid., 131.

9. Ibid., 137.

10. Wilson Harris, "The Fabric of the Imagination", *Third World Quarterly* (January 1990), 178. Subsequent references appear parenthetically in the text.

11. Herman Melville, "Bartleby the Scrivener", *The Piazza Tales* (1856; reprint, Evanston, Ill.: Northwestern–Newberry Edition, 1987), 44.

12. Wilson Harris, *Carnival* (London: Faber and Faber, 1985), 39. Subsequent references appear parenthetically in the text.

13. From a letter from Wilson Harris to Joyce Sparer Adler, written in connection with the Melville Society, February 1985.

14. Wilson Harris, "Benito Cereno", *Enigma of Values* (Aarhus, Denmark: Dangaroo Press, 1975), 46. Subsequent references appear parenthetically in the text.

15. Private notes of conversation between Harris and Adler.

16. Herman Melville, *The Confidence-Man* (1857; reprint, ed. Bruce Franidin, New York: Bobbs-Merrill, 1967), 350.

17. Wilson Harris, "Review of Joyce Sparer Adler's *War in Melville's Imagination*", *Ariel* (April 1982), 84.

18. Private notes of conversation between Harris and Adler.

19. Herman Melville, *Mardi* (1849; reprint, New York: New American Library, 1964), 17.

20. Ibid., 15.

21. Wilson Harris, *The Infinite Rehearsal* (London: Faber and Faber, 1987), 86.

Chapter 9

1. Wilson Harris, *Tradition, the Writer and Society: Critical Essays* (London: New Beacon Publications, 1967), 20.

Bibliography

Bernal, J.D. *Science in History*, Vol. 2. New York: Cameron Associates, 2d ed., 1956.

De Broglie, Louis. *Physics and Microphysics*. New York: Harper, 1960.

Gilbert, Sandra, and Susan Gubar. *The Madwoman in the Attic: The Woman Writer and the Nineteenth-Century Literary Imagination*. New Haven and London: Yale University Press, 2d ed., 2000.

Harris, Wilson. *Heartland*. London: Faber and Faber, 1964.

———. *The Eye of the Scarecrow*. London: Faber and Faber, 1965.

———. *Tradition, the Writer and Society: Critical Essays*. London: New Beacon Publications, 1967.

———. *The Waiting Room*. London: Faber and Faber, 1967.

———. *Tumatumari*. London: Faber and Faber, 1968.

———. *Ascent to Omai*. London: Faber and Faber, 1970.

———. *The Age of the Rainmakers*. London: Faber and Faber, 1971.

———. *Black Marsden*. London: Faber and Faber, 1972.

———. "A Talk on the Subjective Imagination". *New Letters* (Fall 1973).

———. "Benito Cereno". *Enigma of Values*. Aarhus: Dangaroo Press, 1975.

———. *Companions of the Day and Night*. London: Faber and Faber, 1975.

———. *Da Silva da Silva's Cultivated Wilderness [and] Genesis of the Clown*. London: Faber and Faber, 1977.

———. *Eternity to Season*. London: New Beacon Books, 1978.

———. *The Angel at the Gate*. London: Faber and Faber, 1982.

———. "Review of Joyce Sparer Adler's *War in Melville's Imagination*". *Ariel* (April 1982).

———. *The Womb of Space: The Cross-Cultural Imagination*. Westport, Conn.: Greenwood Press, 1983.

———. *Carnival*. London: Faber and Faber, 1985.

———. *Guyana Quartet*. London: Faber and Faber, 1985.

————. *The Infinite Rehearsal*. London: Faber and Faber, 1987.

————. "Comedy and Modern Allegory: A Personal View". In *A Shaping of Connections,* edited by Hena Maes-Jelinek, Kersten Holst Petersen and Anna Rutherford. Coventry: Dangaroo Press, 1989.

————. "The Fabric of the Imagination". *Third World Quarterly* (January 1990).

————. "The Radical Imagination". *Lectures and Talks*. Liege: Département d'Anglais, Université de Liége, 1992.

————. *Jonestown*. London: Faber and Faber, 1996.

Heisenberg, Werner. *Physics and Beyond: Encounters and Conversations*. New York: Harper and Row, 1971.

James, C.L.R. *Mariners, Renegades, and Castaways: The Story of Herman Melville and the World We Live In*. London: Allison and Busby, 1985.

Maes-Jelinek, Hena, ed. *Wilson Harris: The Uncompromising Imagination*. Mundelstrup, Denmark: Dangaroo Press, 1991.

Melville, Herman. *Moby-Dick, or the Whale*. 1851. Reprint, New York: Random House, 1930.

————. *Pierre, or the Ambiguities*. 1852. Reprint, New York: Hendricks House, 1962.

————. *Mardi*. 1849. Reprint, New York: New American Library, 1964.

————. *The Confidence-Man*. 1857. Reprint, edited by Bruce Franidin, New York: Bobbs-Merrill, 1967.

————. "Bartleby the Scrivener", *The Piazza Tales*. 1856. Reprint, Evanston, Ill.: Northwestern–Newberry Edition, 1987.

Monod, Jacques. *Chance and Necessity.* New York: Knopf, 1971.

Munro, Ian, and Reinhard Sander, eds. *Kas-kas: Interviews with Three Caribbean Writers in Texas – George Lamming, C.L.R. James, Wilson Harris*. Austin: African and Afro-American Research Institute, University of Texas at Austin, 1972.

Van Sertima, Ivan. "The Sleeping Rocks". Paper presented at the University of Missouri–Kansas City, 21 June 1973.

Index